The Wheeling Stars

Commander Bill King, DSO and Bar, DSC, was the only submariner in operational command throughout the Second World War. With the coming of peace, he retired from the Royal Navy and married Anita Leslie, a talented historian and biographer, who came from a mildly eccentric family of Anglo-Irish landed gentry. Thereafter he divided his time between farming on the tide-swept shores around Oranmore Castle in County Galway, hunting with the Galway Blazers, and ocean racing – mostly as navigator to John Illingworth in his legendary Fastnet winner, *Myth of Malham*. His delayed honeymoon was spent cruising the Leeward islands in his 24-foot ketch *Galway Blazer* with Anita and baby Tarka as crew, all recorded in her light-hearted book, *Love in a Nutshell*.

But Bill King's wartime nightmares were not finally exorcized until he sailed his 42-foot junk-rigged *Galway Blazer II* around the world alone. The circumnavigation took nearly three years, thanks to being rolled over and dismasted in the South Atlantic and all but sunk by a hostile sea-monster south of Australia. He was sixty-two by the time he rode again with the Blazers. At the age of seventy-eight he took up hang-gliding with a first flight off a 10,000-foot peak in the French Alps.

THE
WHEELING STARS

A Guide for
Lone Sailors

Bill King

faber and faber

LONDON · BOSTON

First published in 1989
by Faber and Faber Limited
3 Queen Square London WCIN 3AU

Phototypeset by Input Typesetting Ltd, London
Printed in Great Britain by
Richard Clay Ltd, Bungay, Suffolk

© Bill King, 1989

Foreword © Mike Richey, 1989

A CIP record for this book is available from the British Library

ISBN 0–571–15396–8

For
Anita, beloved wife, mother and grandmother,
and
'Blondie' Hasler, splendid friend, mariner and warrior.

'In life their sparkle was never dimmed,
Nor after death was their memory.'

Bill King in the cockpit of *Galway Blazer II* with
a one-panel reef in each sail.

Contents

List of illustrations

Foreword
by Mike Richey

Bill King, I have always thought, belongs among the immortals. His voyage round the world alone, dogged as it was by setbacks of one kind and another, set no records (except, I suppose, doubling the Horn under junk rig); but it had an epic quality to it, perhaps because it was in part a catharsis for the long gruelling years he spent in the submarine service during the war. He wrote about it in what one might call a seamanlike fashion but occasionally there would be a ring of the allegorical – as in Melville. But unlike Melville he does not contemplate the whiteness of the great shark that stove his boat in but rather considers the colour of anti-fouling least likely to provoke attack from such monsters. For Bill, for all his mystical side, is very much the practical seaman and his writings are full of sound advice.

In the present volume he ruminates over a lifetime of seafaring and takes the reader on a fairly random voyage of discovery, from freak seas on the continental shelf to the lone sailor's sixth sense, or magnetic anomalies off Bermuda to living on almond paste and Mung beans. No voyager could wish for a better companion. *Bon voyage!*

Preface

I intended that this book should be mainly philosophical and descriptive; that there should be few scientific explanations or lists of things to do or take with you. I set out with no intention of writing any form of handbook or technical reference manual. Like many good resolutions, these have not been entirely fulfilled.

None the less, the objective has been kept in view, which is to stimulate your thoughts and bring you into the very heart of the adventure of sailing alone. Perhaps you may find yourself in your imagination, if not in fact, alone in a small boat crossing a trackless and turbulent ocean.

Much of what I have written is equally applicable to those who sail short-handed or with inexperienced crews.

> The man who rounds the Horn
> Aboard a leaking shell
> Afloat in monster seas
> Alone with his stray thoughts
> For company
>
> Knows more than kings
> With crowns, or navigators
> Of steel ships:
> He senses in his salt-cracked brain
> The force that splits the ocean.
> Lionel Leslie (1900–86)

Acknowledgements

Thanks are due to the following for permission to use quoted material: William Kimber and Co Ltd for *Dive and Attack* by Bill King; Nautical Books for *Adventure in Depth* by Bill King; Leonie Monteiro de Barros for the poem by her father, the late Lionel Leslie, on page xiii; HMSO for *Meto. 895, Meteorology for Mariners* (third edition); Hutchinson & Co Ltd for *Francis Chichester* by Anita Leslie.

The line drawing on page 19 is by Leonard Clow and those on pages 38 and 39 by Time Life with subsequent corrections by Graham Parrish.

CHAPTER ONE

Introduction

Me miserum quanti
montes volvuntur aquarum

The Latin lesson dimly remembered over a gap of nearly seventy years is, I think, a couplet of a verse from a poem by Ovid. A rough translation of the whole verse is, I recall,

> Woe is me; wheresoever I look there is naught but sea and sky
> Mountainous waves roll threateningly around me.

Ovid had reason to dread his situation. He was a landsman. He was on a sea voyage to his place of banishment from Rome. In those days even seamen became edgy when out of sight of land, for navigation was sketchy. Finally those great swells appeared to rush towards the frail craft. The true nature of wave motion, the circular movement of water particles, was almost certainly not understood by the despairing poet. Perhaps he was seasick, poor fellow. All these various thoughts do occur to many people, and I have frequently been questioned about single-handed long-distance voyages – Why do people, why do *you* do it? Is not life already sufficiently difficult without making it more so? Either because it is a complex question, or because I have a grasshopper mind, I have found myself giving a different answer each time. So, one day, while travelling across the central Irish bog in a train, with the clack-clack-diddlydah of the wheels in my ears, I put down my answer in verse; well, if not a reason it is at least an excuse:

> The breathless beauty of the wheeling stars,
> The flaming glory of the northern lights,

The muted thunder in a doldrum cloud,
Piled up, evolving, undershot by sun.
Sailor give hail,
These works are your bounty,
And your grail.

This introduction is to introduce myself to you, the reader, for thus you may be able to evaluate what you later read. At the age of seventy-eight I am able to write objectively about myself, without boastfulness or false modesty.

I have met a few very audacious people; fought alongside them in war, sailed with them across oceans, ski'd and climbed with them over mountains. I have admired and envied them, but have never been able to emulate them. I was cast in a super-cautious mould. You, the reader, are, I think, fortunate to have super-cautious advice, for thus you may be warned of pitfalls, but be free to temper my caution with your audacity.

From some emotional urge, I joined the Royal Navy as an officer-cadet at the age of thirteen and found later that I was totally unsuited to this profession. The requirements are, in my view, good health and physique, a decisive and executive mind, a gregarious nature and a fair amount of technical ability. A square peg in a round hole is an uncomfortable notion. None the less it will fit, provided that the corner-to-corner distance of the square is less than the diameter of the hole: some discomfort, however, remains.

I recall that my great grandfather was an eminent palaeontologist – a dedicated student of prehistoric creatures. Did my talents perhaps lie within some ivory tower where problems could be investigated at length and in depth? This will never be known for I remained obstinately square in my round hole, and indeed went farther down the round hole into the submarine service.

Seamanship is, like surgery, a branch of engineering: the resolution of forces, the putting together of physical situations – what else? common sense, some manual dexterity and, finally, experience. I pitifully recall myself in the Seamanship Room at the Royal Naval College, Dartmouth, fumbling with a bowline knot which came undone when everyone else's held.

To be a good navigator one should be a reasonably able mathematician, a fast and accurate arithmetician and have good calligraphy. To me mathematics was a half-closed book – I can't count the change and my handwriting is like the proverbial drunken spider's trail. Do not, I beg you, despair if you find yourself in a similar situation.

'How', you may ask, 'did the fellow get across the oceans if he was such a bad seaman and navigator?' Well, I was blessed by a number of fortunate chances and sailed with a series of brilliantly competent skippers who made it all look easy. To anyone familiar with the sailing world, their names are like a peal of trumpets in the Halls of Fame: John Illingworth, the crack ocean-racing skipper of the years immediately following the Second World War; Blondie Hasler, a brilliant ocean sailor and marine inventor; Humphrey Barton, under whose tuition I learned the art of mastheading in a mid-Atlantic gale to repair broken standing rigging; Bobby Somerset, so experienced that he seemed part of the sea and its moods; Bobby Lowein, of splendid physique, equally able as afterguard or on the foredeck; Peter Haward, a pioneer professional yacht delivery man who has sailed more thousands of miles than most people have had hot dinners, and Mike Mason, high adventurer and sailor.

From all these great men with whom I sailed something rubbed off on me. 'Still,' you may enquire, 'with so few natural attributes, why did he not stay on land?' Nature gives with one hand as she takes away with the other. I was born with a lifelong total immunity from seasickness and discovered that I was also immune to loneliness (more of this later). Also I spent a great deal of my leisure skiing and riding horses. The practice of these sports accustoms one to balance, keeping the centre of gravity over the point of support, allowing for acceleration or retardation, and the clamping of the lower part of the body to a moving object while the upper part remains freely poised. This is how you take a celestial navigational sight while your small boat is riding the crest of a Southern Ocean greybeard wave.

Anyone wishing to advance their maritime efficiency should first browse in marine bookshops or libraries and read the step-by-step instruction books. Second, if possible try to get a friend to teach you to sail a dinghy.

Third, sign on as crew with one of the yacht-delivery firms: the skippers usually sail with some experienced crews, but also with young people who are in the apprentice stage. They will be your 'sea daddies', I hope. All one needs is humility, an enquiring mind and a discipline for learning. The sea also exerts its own discipline. Finally, I commend to your notice Murphy's Laws, which govern so much of the human situation.

Murphy's First Law is widely known and evolves from the cussedness of inanimate objects and the random factor of the universe:

1   If anything can go wrong, it will.

The laws which follow from this are perhaps not so familiar:

2   Nothing is quite so bad as it seems.

3   If anything does go wrong, it is usually your own fault.

Finally, Murphy's Fourth Law:

4   In this life nothing is fair or unfair, *Things are.*

CHAPTER TWO

Ethics of
the Lone Sailor

I remember, not long ago, there was a strong editorial campaign in a yachting magazine denouncing the concept of sailing alone.

Primarily the argument was that the fundamental rule of the International Regulations for Preventing Collisions at Sea is that vessels under way should at all times keep a good look out. Sooner or later the lone mariner must sleep and, therefore, disobey this rule. At first sight this argument is unanswerable – so let me answer it.

THE POTENTIAL THREAT TO OTHERS
OF A SINGLEHANDED SAILOR

I think that the monsters which are sometimes entered for singlehanded races pose such a threat of damage to others in case of collision that they are an unjustifiable risk. The man who goes out alone to fish in a rowing boat can be said to pose no threat, and a small light craft, which is all that a lone mariner requires, will, if she is run down by a seagoing vessel, probably be hardly noticed. The risk is accepted by the mariner alone. Coasting, however, is a different matter; other small vessels are liable to be encountered; the voyage which may have been planned to be of short duration may become extended by the onset of fog or heavy weather; in this case the mariner will either have to sleep or will become less vigilant.

I planned my voyage round the world in 1969 to start from Plymouth. Thus, I thought I should be well up to windward of Ushant and able to take a course down mid-Channel, clear of shipping lanes and fishing banks. As the boat was built at Cowes it was necessary to sail the 200 miles or so to the start line. Thinking how puny this little trip was I went off alone. As we left the Solent fog came down and the wind fell light. I coasted nervously along the shipping lanes; the ships' sirens moaned continuously like a herd of wounded elephants. For one moment the curtain cleared into wisps of mist as the biggest tanker in the world shot close across my bows, its passage through the gap seemed eternal.

The voyage took at least forty-eight hours during which time I had not one wink of rest. Next time I did a similar voyage after my return, I took a friend with me. Plenty of people do coast single-handed successfully, but I now think that one should not do so. Likewise the return to a landfall should be carefully planned to pose the least danger. One of the early basic rules of navigation is 'When making a landfall on an unfamiliar coast or in poor visibility, do not edge in to the coast: stand well off and make your landfall at right angles to the coastline. If necessary, wait for daylight or improvement in visibility.' This advice has enormously increased impact on a lone voyager with limited vigilance. No single-handed race should finish with a course which brushes up along the coastline.

SAFETY AIDS

Recent developments of sensors are producing more safety measures which do the looking out. A radar which, perhaps, squeaks when a target is found; a passive receiver which registers the radar emissions of another vessel provided that it is on the same frequency; these are expensive, require some form of battery charger and are not trouble free, but the great leap forward is the new radar reflector. It looks like a sausage, and I was told that its interior is like a Brillo pad; anyhow it apparently gives a massive blip on a ship's radar tube. Using one during a recent voyage I found that enormous tankers in low visibility would stop, puzzled that they had an apparently large vessel on their screen when the yacht was invisible to them.

THE LONE SAILOR'S SIXTH SENSE

Now I come to the difficult part – the realm of paranormality. I early adopted a philosophy of non-belief in the unseen – things such as ghosts and poltergeists. However, during my lone voyages, sailing unlit on dark nights and asleep, I worked a routine of waking up every two hours to review the general situation and to make certain no other vessels were endangering me. I found, however, that I would sometimes wake up out of routine and go on deck to find the lights of a ship approaching me. This seemed to occur too frequently to be a coincidence. On none of my routine checks did I sight anything.

In the Southern Ocean other ships are rarely encountered, but one night I found myself stumbling towards the hatch. My horrified gaze met a maze of lights close aboard.

Eyes dazed by sleep focused on a red light to port of me; she was passing clear. A few more blinks cleared my vision; there were *two* red lights indicating a vessel not under control, and among the glitter of working lights, a dim green glow, a *starboard* light. We were actually closing rapidly on a collision course. I tacked, gulping with fear and slid under her stern – why in all this vast empty ocean had I the misfortune to cross tracks with a whaling fleet's mother ship towing dead whales? Thank God for whatever alarm system awoke me.

On return to land, I mentioned these facts to a very prestigious mariner. 'Oh,' he said, 'we all accept this.' I did not quite elucidate who 'we' were or what 'this' was exactly. Later, browsing around a publisher's office I noticed a copy of Arthur Koestler's *The Roots of Coincidence*. A whole new world unfolded and perhaps explained my experiences. To shorten a long treatise into a few sentences, this is what seems to happen according to conclusions from a broad spectrum of scientific disciplines. People or possibly even objects give off emanations. These are probably so minute that they cannot yet be classified as either waves or particles. They probably have no mass. They travel at very high speed and may impinge on some of the millions of brain cells of a sleeping but alert human being. Believe this or not, but if you are interested, the subject rewards study.

THE NEUTRINO

The possibility of the existence of such emanations seems to evolve from the discovery of the neutrino. This, the smallest-known particle, has no apparent mass or electric charge, can scarcely be classified as either particle or wave and has the ability to pass through whatever matter it encounters. It only meets its Waterloo when it collides with another neutrino; then both disintegrate into gamma rays.

Many years have passed since all this came to my notice and research advances science continuously. The physicist and psychologist have come close together in this field and investigation into precognition and extra-sensory perception indicates the possibility of mind-originated transmissions which may be transferable to others.

Constant vigilance is a near impossibility. During many years of submarine warfare I found that when the submarine was on the surface, lookouts, whose own lives and those of their crewmates depended on total vigilance during their watch, would frequently relapse into a semi-somnolent daze and had to be constantly kept up to the mark. Military sentries, with a death penalty threatening them for failure, have frequently fallen asleep. Two would be required to ensure each other's wakefulness.

My experience of modern merchant ships very close to one's boat is that the average standard of lookout is very poor. Recently I found a medium-sized vessel coming up astern and threatening to run us down. Her ambulatory steering made it difficult to avoid her. Firing flares failed to attract attention, but eventually I raised her on VHF radio and begged her, by roaring, to go away.

To sum up: a proper organization will bring the mariner into a state of equal vigilance with other ocean users and he will be of little threat to anyone except, perhaps, another lone sailor.

CHAPTER THREE

Fear and Loneliness

'Cowards die many times before their deaths;
The valiant never taste of death but once'
Shakespeare

FEAR

I can claim to have notched up a record number of premature deaths along those lines and am, therefore, uniquely qualified to address you on the subject of fear.

Let us explore for a moment the direct opposite, or perhaps the conquest of fear – military valour. This can be indoctrinated into whole communities. The Samurai, the upper-caste warriors of Old Japan, somewhat like the Scottish Highland clansmen, were imbued with the precepts of courage, honour and loyalty, particularly total loyalty to their overlord or chief, the Daimyo. They had to excel in martial arts and give their lives in battle without thought of surrender. Like the Scots, most of their fighting was in inter-clan warfare (until 1608 when the Shogun imposed order).

In 1868 the God-Emperor Mutsu Hito, realizing that Japan was threatened with extinction by the better-organized Western powers, assumed the temporal authority and abolished the clan feudal system. All Japanese – farmers, merchants, artisans, even the untouchables – were made available for induction into a national army and navy.

The Samurai Code, Bushido, was imposed on all; not, one imagines, without a certain amount of nastiness on the part of the sergeants. None the less this was achieved; the modern Japanese army would fight to the last man and the last bullet. In the Second World War there were very, very few unwounded Japanese prisoners of war.

9

Many fanatical religious sects show the same total disregard of death. So it is possible for ordinary folk to become heroic? But while remembering this fact, let us not, I suggest, think of emulating the process. Let us study the subject of fear in an objective fashion.

There are three types of fear which I shall deal with in turn.

Anxiety or Worry

This is where one sits grinding one's ulcers: worrying about whether the wife is having it off with someone else, if the children are going to drop out or if one's career, stocks and shares or job will collapse. All these may never happen; but what is it like in the eye of a hurricane? What is the weather forecast for Cape Horn?

A friend, with whom I used to ski, would stay up roistering in night-clubs until 3 a.m. and then catch the 9 a.m. bus to the ski slopes. He was eighty-four. I asked him, 'What is the secret of being an octogenarian teenager?' He considered briefly and replied in a convincing manner, 'I eat little, I eat slowly and I *never* worry.'

I had noticed that his feeding habits were little different from mine; but, as a compulsive worrier, his last rule had a tremendous impact on me. I had often read psychological treatises on the desirability of avoiding worry, all of which slid off my back, but here in front of me was a living testimony. It dawned on me that, since worry is a long-term problem and a purely destructive factor it should be possible to tackle it by an accelerating mental effort, for the sake of one's health and happiness and for the success of one's adventures.

Panic

Panic is the second state of fear. This is when mentally or physically you flap around like a wet hen. A man under heavy fire has perhaps two panic buttons: he presses one, runs away and is shot for cowardice, or presses the other and wins a posthumous decoration. The correct action might have been an orderly retreat or a flanking attack. Before I lecture you on what to do, let me assure you that if, like me, you lose your head when all about you are keeping theirs, the very fact that when you are alone there are no annoying people around keeping their heads does encourage one to keep one's own. The ideal reaction to an emergency is the shot of adrenalin which gives the necessary energy to master the situation. The response should be to recognize the onset of panic and consciously *slow down*.

Relax, perhaps by letting your tongue fill your mouth. When you are tensed with panic it presses up on the hard palate. Actually you will still be working at top speed, but in a 'controlled fashion' with adrenalin pumping.

Despair

The last enemy is despair. Then you collapse, perhaps in the foetal position, and let disaster wash over you. At this point a restatement of Murphy's Second Law cannot be too strongly emphasized. 'Nothing is quite so bad as it seems.' You may exclaim, 'Supposing disaster is inevitable; you have perhaps fallen out of an aircraft with no parachute.' Well, here is where Murphy's Law conjoins with the Christian message: let the last few seconds be happy! Despair is, however, normally a slow process and this gives time for contemplation, a reassessment of the situation and the possible options still open to you.

My experience of having a hole knocked into the bottom of my boat in mid-ocean by a cousin of 'Jaws' taught me that all those three types of fear can arrive in close succession, and this does complicate the scene. They do, however, attack at different moments in time, and can be recognized and tackled separately.

To sum up: for *panic* slow down, contemplate and analyse; for *worry* and *despair* speed up and optimize. Much of this I intend to develop along practical lines in a later chapter 'Disasters'.

LONELINESS

(i) 'Thou shalt love thy neighbour as thyself'
(Second commandment of Jesus Christ; which even from an agnostic's point of view is very hard to fault).
(ii) 'No man is an island entire of itself' (John Donne).

When, however, you sail alone through the Southern Ocean you have *no* neighbours, sometimes for a distance of two thousand miles. Also you *are* an island of yourself. These facts should, I think, be kept in mind, and I shall pursue the matter later in this chapter.

Some people have very firmly inbuilt mental allergies which must be respected. If you are claustrophobic, do not volunteer for submarine service. If you have vertigo, go to the top of the Jungfrau by the mountain railway rather than climb the north face of the Eiger. If you suffer from agoraphobia (fear of open spaces or, literally, of market places) do not take a job at the check-out counter of the supermarket.

Some people do not like being alone for five minutes. Gavin Maxwell, the 'otter man', wrote that one of his aunts had announced, 'I cannot think *why* solitary confinement is considered a punishment; for me it would be absolute bliss.' These are the extremes.

There is a hard and fast rule that if you go mountain climbing, you must never go alone. I confess that I have disobeyed this rule many times in the last sixty years. I considered that, with a proper map and compass and with my natural agility and super-cautious nature, there was no reasonable cause for trepidation, nor a situation in which the rescue services would be called upon. I saw the folly of my ways on a nine-thousand-foot volcano in New Zealand. As I attained the glacier, crater lake and summit, a blizzard set in. I confidently took out my compass only to find that the core of the mountain was magnetized and the compass tried to point down at it and jammed. Apart from that foolishness, I discovered that I never felt lonely when alone and this characteristic continued to benefit me on long, lone, ocean voyages.

To discover one's own reactions to being alone one should ideally do a medium-distance sail of, say, 500 to 1,000 miles: then if you find you have a real mental allergy to being alone you will discover it and save yourself much suffering and possibly disaster.

Someone wrote, perhaps too optimistically, 'No man can be lonely when alone with his Maker.' For those for whom this is not enough companionship there is the ever-changing sea and sky, which form a stage and a backdrop for the vast variety of fish, marine mammals and the concourse of birds which pass by, come to visit you briefly or follow your boat for considerable periods of time. I shall discuss these aspects of lone voyaging in more detail in a later chapter.

All these, if not your neighbours, are at least in your neighbourhood.

The outside opinion from people close to me of my seeming immunity from loneliness has been: 'He is so damned pleased with himself' and again, 'His memory is so bad that he can't remember if he has been at sea for three minutes or three years.' There may be truth in all this, but I would add that I am not naturally gregarious; I do not shine in the fellowship of club, pub or cocktail party. Also, I had the experience of commanding operational submarines almost continuously throughout the Second World War. Although I was surrounded by a high-density population in a small enclosed environment, the responsibility of lone command while also standing in for doctor and priest, frequently out of touch with superior control, imposed on me an isolated personality; a training perhaps for lone adventure.

Now you may well come to the conclusion that, as I have had a lot of fear I am well qualified to talk on that subject, but that, as I don't feel loneliness, I am not an expert in that field.

Having had considerable experience of being alone I have realized that concentrating on one objective or task with which you are totally familiar will result in a slow mental deterioration; and this perhaps is a sinister facet of loneliness or could be its trigger.

A substitute for your neighbour, a bridge from the 'island of yourself' can be found in the written words of people of high intelligence. Normally I have just time to read a horror comic on a journey or for five minutes before sleep, but for my voyage round the world, I embarked a library of paperbacks, which did not quite last the course. When I ran short of books, I perceived a lapse into a slack mentality.

BOOKS TO TAKE ON A LONE VOYAGE

I started by reading the New Testament from cover to cover. I was brought up as a traditionalist in the Church of England and Royal Navy. 'Fear God, honour the King, tell the truth, serve out the rum.' I recall an article in the King's Regulations and Admiralty Instructions which described some crime as being: 'To the derogation of God's honour and to the prejudice of good order and naval discipline.' The two phrases became synonymous for me.

From these precepts flowed religious observance and the moral code. Looking at the New Testament objectively, or so I thought, I found that, apart from a few pieces which I could not understand, the whole document had the undoubted ring of truth. Many of you may belong to other religions or to no religion at all, but for those who cannot accept the divine source and intervention I recommend it as an enormously interesting philosophical study.

Moving from my own to comparative religion I read the Koran and a treatise on Zen Buddhism. Thus one discovers the well-springs of belief of people of other faiths. I also took, as a sequence in time, the works of some of the best-known philosophers. They included Socrates, Plato, Aristotle, Julius Caesar, Marcus Aurelius, Seneca, Boethius, Pascal, Descartes, the Duc de St Simon and Matthew Arnold. All these were interspersed with novels by writers who had previously been vaguely remembered names. This list included Chekhov, Tolstoy, Gogol, Turgenev, Dostoevsky, Trollope, Henry James, Virginia Woolf, Proust, Zola, Voltaire and Balzac; also some ancient Greek plays translated by Paul Roche into English verse; the Sonnets of Shakespeare, and a few which I forget. I selected my library by browsing in some good bookshops mostly in the classical and philosophical sections. I spent a lot of time on this and very great was my reward.

On my return I talked with a great intellectual, perhaps rather boastfully after a couple of drinks, about my advance into the scholastic field. I quickly realized that whereas I had been doing it for a year or so, he had done it for fifty years. Rather like boasting about one's boxing prowess to Barry McGuigan, as I might have been tempted to do, solely because I was once a reluctant runner-up in the Mediterranean Fleet championship at exactly the same weight.

To sum up: one's reaction to loneliness should be carefully monitored, and can be alleviated by spiritual or mental activity and by the aesthetic enjoyment of your surroundings.

CHAPTER FOUR

Navigation

THE BEDROCK – CELESTIAL NAVIGATION

On joining the British fleet in 1927 I was painfully introduced to the black art of celestial navigation. The observations of the sun, moon and stars were by a complicated mathematical process rendered into position lines, which, when crossed at suitable angles, would indicate a position. This process involved looking up a large number of factors in Inman's seven-figure tables and then doing a vast number of additions and subtractions. The process seemed to take me for ever. During this lengthy period, I would make arithmetical errors which meant that the sums had to be done again and again. The time now taken had risen to for ever squared. To fix the position from the stars one had, if possible, to measure the altitude of at least three of them. We are now considering the time spent in their computation as three times for ever squared; well beyond the practical limits imposed by shipboard routine.

I was careful not to try to enrol in the specialist navigation branch, but when I eventually commanded submarines in wartime I was glad to find that my navigators were frequently Merchant Service officers with vast experience of celestial navigation and that the Merchant Service used a method of calculation which was a far shorter cut to the answer. The Admiralty had rejected this method on the grounds of insufficient accuracy.

Many years after that war I discovered from a friend who commanded destroyers in conditions of almost continuous wartime action that, realizing the impossibility of allocating a sufficient amount of anybody's time to long calculations, he had found that the RAF used an even quicker method than the Merchant Service which was even more heavily frowned on by the Admiralty. Now I can see why their Lordships insisted on the old-fashioned methods in a big ship with qualified navigating officers and their assistants working in relatively dry and steady platforms.

A destroyer, however, tossing in heavy seas with the commanding and other officers on continuous alert and watches, was in a different category. My friend 'borrowed' some RAF tables and used them to good account and with adequate accuracy.

On leaving the Royal Navy, shortly after the war ended, I joined the crew of John Illingworth's yacht, *Myth of Malham*, as navigator. In view of my past experience, and of John's considerable reputation as a race-winner, I did this with some trepidation and not without demurring.

I had, however, developed an immense keenness to join the ocean-racing world, in spite of my physique which, as a wispy long-distance runner, fell far short of the requirements for what is now known as a 'foredeck gorilla'. As navigator I was getting in by the back door, but a pretty stiff back door.

John, then the star of the ocean-racing world, wished to know his position every quarter of an hour to reassess his strategy. He expected to meet the course markers bang on the nose.

When the skies were clear I took observations of dawn stars, morning sun, a meridian altitude sight at noon, afternoon sun and dusk stars, working these out by the only method I knew, the Inman's seven-figure tables which I had previously considered beyond me. The dusk stars had to be worked out by dim cabin light with the boat perhaps slamming hard to windward.

When skies were obscured, an accurate up-to-the-minute estimated position had to be kept: this method will be pursued later in this chapter.

I found that the immense impetus of my new ambition, combined with the enthusiastic drive of the skipper and the infectious keenness of an expert crew in a winning vein imposed on me enough discipline to master the situation. I settled down to a new professionalism. I also had time, and only just time, to study the ocean-racing strategy of a master, to watch some very expert helmsmanship at close quarters and to see the controlled antics of sail handlers and repair work at sea. I hope that the reason for dragging you through these personal reminiscences will become apparent.

If you have an ambition to sail the ocean, with others or alone, and feel that the expertise of navigation is beyond you do not despair – a lesser man than you has made it. Furthermore, you will find from what follows that the task has been much eased. It took a woman, Mary Blewitt, to lighten the toil of the yachtsman.

Mary Blewitt was a WAAF in the Second World War. During periods of boredom she taught herself navigation from the manuals. She became navigator of *Myth of Malham* when I departed for Ireland after two seasons in the chair. She subsequently wrote a book *Celestial Navigation for Yachtsmen* which is based on those forbidden RAF tables used by my friend in his destroyer. This method reduces the time taken to work out a sight to a few minutes; using a modern pocket calculator it becomes seconds.

In 1969 when I prepared to sail *Galway Blazer II* round the world I was delighted to hear of this new handbook. I fear that it disobeys the rule governing handbooks, being totally explicit and comprehensible, with none of the usual abstract verbiage which freezes the brain and is frequently found to be inaccurate. The whole mystery of celestial navigation is unveiled in all its simplicity.

RADIO AIDS

There are, in this highly technological age, many electronic and radionic aids to navigation which give one an accurate position at the press of a button. Remembering, however, that they are expensive, liable to break down and use up limited battery power, do not, I beg of you, neglect your celestial navigation. With sufficient practice one can use the position obtained by the sextant to thread between unlit islands in the middle of a stormy, pitch-black night south of Tierra del Fuego.

CARE AND TECHNIQUES OF SEXTANT WORK

Now I come to the weak point of my argument. I mentioned the fallibility of press-button gadgetry. What about the sextant? It is a very delicate instrument. If the mirrors are knocked, considerable errors will immediately be built in. These are the precautions which you must take:

1 Treat your sextant with the care which you would lavish on a new-born baby. See that its stowage is so secure that were the boat to cartwheel the sextant would remain immobile in its box.
2 When you are moving up on deck or returning to the cabin, and while taking your sights, move with exaggerated caution and balance. Keep yourself defensive against sudden movement, but do not let your care for the instrument expose you to the risk of falling overboard. Clip on your safety line before coming on deck and unclip after returning below. Always have your safety line on a short span so that you cannot fall far.
3 Learn and practice the method of correcting the errors of the sextant; so if you do give it an inadvertent knock, you can quickly correct it.
4 Each time you take a sight make a rough check for errors beforehand.

If you are going on a long voyage, take a spare sextant. It could be one of the cheap plastic type.

Now, all I have said in this chapter is of general application to small-boat sailing. If you are alone, it becomes even more important. You have no one you can ask to check your observations and workings. The art of bringing down the heavenly body in one half of the mirror to the sea horizon in the other half is that much more difficult when you are alone.

It is, of course, necessary to take the sight on or near the crest of the wave or swell. If you take a sight from the trough of a big wave you will measure the altitude not from the horizon but from the nearest crest. An enormous error will ensue, which may transfer your position from the Atlantic to inside Canterbury Cathedral. I used to get a crewmate to whisper into my ear 'trough, trough, coming up crest, crest' and to help warn me of a breaking crest which would turn the boat into a cocktail shaker and drench the sextant. Alone, you must learn to feel all this with the seat of your pants. The instructions about falling over the side become more important. You

Opposite Hull drawing of *Galway Blazer II*.

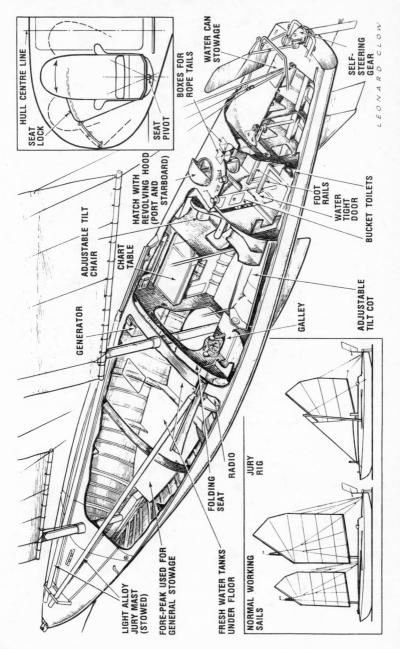

HULL CENTRE LINE

SEAT LOCK

SEAT PIVOT

BOXES FOR ROPE TAILS

WATER CAN STOWAGE

SELF-STEERING GEAR

LEONARD CLOW

ADJUSTABLE TILT CHAIR

HATCH WITH REVOLVING HOOD (PORT AND STARBOARD)

CHART TABLE

FOOT RAILS

WATER TIGHT DOOR

BUCKET TOILETS

GENERATOR

GALLEY

ADJUSTABLE TILT COT

RADIO

FOLDING SEAT

JURY RIG

LIGHT ALLOY JURY MAST (STOWED)

FORE-PEAK USED FOR GENERAL STOWAGE

FRESH WATER TANKS UNDER FLOOR

NORMAL WORKING SAILS

19

have no one to write down your time and altitude. You must note and memorize the time on your watch or clip a stopwatch which was started at a noted time. It is general practice to take a series of sights; but I have found that it is better to develop such practised confidence that you can rely on one observation. Now some of my own experiences can usefully be quoted.

Come with me for a short while, backwards in time to 4 February 1972 and southwards to the latitude of Drake Passage between South America and Antarctica. We are on the deck of *Galway Blazer II*, a 4½-ton junk of ultra-light construction.

The general weather pattern is dictated by a family of depressions passing rapidly south of us, trailing their associated warm and cold front across our track. I have been keeping a meticulous line of celestial navigational positions across the South Pacific and Southern Oceans. It is forty-four days since we crossed the longitude of Tasmania, just about a record passage. If we keep up this cracking pace we shall pass between the unlit island outposts of Diego Ramirez and Ildefonso tonight, and round Cape Horn tomorrow. I am fairly confident of the navigation; my observed positions have slotted in well with those estimated; the current runs at nearly a knot with us.

A wet warm front went over during last night and we are in the drier westerly winds between that and the approaching cold front. With steady strong winds of about Force 8–9, and in deep water, the seas are running in firm sinusoidal curves. Their breaking crests are not waterfalling down their fronts. The spume is sliding down their backs in white water and veined patterns.

The sky is overcast and I desperately want a noon sight for latitude, to give a position line which I can run along in the night with dark rocks seven miles either side of me. I reflect that it is surprising how frequently the sun shows itself at local noon; it sort of burns through, I suppose.

The mainsail is stowed and we are running with one panel of the foresail set. The wind is blowing about 45 knots, but as we are going at maximum speed, there is not much more than 35 knots over the deck. I jam my legs and centre of gravity around the boom crutch and the stowed mainsail, my safety line clipped on and at short stay, like a monkey's tail round a branch.

As I check the sextant for errors, it seems, after so much practice, to be an extension of myself. I preset the calculated angle of the sun's altitude and await the approaching time of apparent noon. Sure enough there is a light up behind the veils of cloud. Out comes the sun. In case I am denied a shot at exact noon I take a quick timed shot which will give me a good approximation, although not the perfection which I desire. This means I have to unhitch myself, dart below to record the time and altitude and get back into position.

The waves are running probably with a significant height of 8 metres and a period of about 8 seconds. The sight must be taken near the crest of the wave and just before it breaks when the boat shakes violently and the sextant is whisked into a cave in the lower part of my anorak, out of the spray: well, you might just catch a sight after the breaker, just before you subside out of sight of the horizon. The wave motion is monitored by my subconscious mind.

The sun is in and out, but the glorious thing is, it hangs in mid-air a while, between rising to its meridian passage and sinking back towards the night. Thank God we have it! Steady, firm, clear, and stopped. The next sight shows a slight fall.

Down below the latitude is plotted, tonight we shall run between the islands. In actuality so we did, under bare masts in a storm-force shriek from the Pole and without sighting the rocky shores; but I shall not keep you with me to share my trepidation.

NAVIGATION BY DEAD RECKONING AND ESTIMATION

It is fairly simple to lay off your course and distance made good from your known speed, but, alas, the ocean also moves.

On the continental shelf the tidal streams may be readily calculated from information given in the charts and tide tables. It is all too easy, however, to make a rough general sweep of the tendency over the area, especially if you have all the other ship's duties on your hands. You must discipline yourself to calculate each hourly set for the position which you occupy at that hour and plot it. Try both methods and you will find a sharp difference in accuracy.

Surface drift, frequently confused with leeway, is the other ocean movement and this is far less predictable than the tidal streams. The friction of the wind currents drives the water with it; albeit at a slower pace than the wind. In areas where there is a steady prevailing wind, the surface drift is a fairly constant ocean current and is forecast with a fair degree of accuracy in the Ocean Pilot charts. Local and fluctuating winds produce their own surface drift and this, which is frequently confused with leeway, must be carefully appreciated and calculated and, if necessary, superimposed on the known ocean current.

Surface drift depends on the strength of the wind, the fetch over which it blows and the time span for which it continues. Incidentally it relates to wave motion which has the same factors. These factors can never be accurately known by a single observer at sea, and from this fact stems much of the·inaccuracy of an estimated position and the desirability of celestial navigation or whatever position-finding gadgetry you can afford.

My experience of surface drift is that a hurricane-force wind blowing for twelve to twenty-four hours will set the water moving at about 3 knots. The ordinary south-wester in the Channel around Force 7 will after, say, six hours, drift you at about half a knot, rising to three-quarters of a knot if it continues to blow.

The drift, although abating, will continue for a while when the wind has gone down. But you must remember that, if you set out in a calm or light easterly and if it has only just stopped blowing a sou'wester, you will be in the grip of the drift from the earlier wind for about three hours.

Water movement is, of course, of immense importance to a mariner in a small, somewhat slow-moving sailing boat as the current or drift is a large factor relative to the boat's speed through the water.

To return to the factor of leeway: I found when navigating *Myth of Malham* that a yacht with a good keel-grip of the water and sailing at a good pace will make little leeway. In fact, while trying carefully to monitor tidal streams, ocean current and local surface drift I regarded leeway as negligible; we seemed to make our landfalls on the nose without allowing for any. Boats with shallow keels do, of course, make leeway. My experience in this type of hull was a catamaran with a broken leeboard which we needed to sail to windward for 1,300 miles; a lot of sideways sailing ensued. The angle of leeway can be observed by noting the angle which the yacht's wake makes to the fore-and-aft line when steering a steady course. I find this a fairly difficult judgement owing to the vagaries of steering.

When recording one's course it is vitally important to log the course actually steered rather than the course ordered to be followed. When navigating ocean racers, I used to badger the helmsman into recording his actual average course steered over each hour; sometimes a difficult admission. The importance of this is further enhanced when sailing as close to the wind as possible.

The expert helmsman will nose up to slice through each wave crest and bear away on top to get maximum acceleration to overcome the backward-moving trough and the smack of the next breaking crest. Thus he works up to windward; but you, the navigator, must know how far. If you are alone you must constantly spy on your self-steering system and monitor its achievements.

When sailing alone from Plymouth across the Bay of Biscay and southwards past the Iberian peninsular I kept three plots going. The estimated position, the position by celestial navigation, and the position by Consol – a system which only requires a radio receiver and a special chart, but which is now, I understand, obsolete.

I was finally satisfied and delighted when, after a lot of practice, all three positions dropped into a single point. *Olé!*

I have emphasized in all this the importance of expertise, practice and pin-point accuracy in the field of navigation, particularly when you are close to land or shallowing water. I have an idea, however, that if you do your homework thoroughly, you may occasionally glimpse a view of the divine madness which could home you in when circumstances are pressing.

I was navigating *Myth of Malham* during the Fastnet Race of 1947 for John Illingworth, at that time the tiger of the seas. We were returning to Plymouth after rounding the lonely rock off the Irish coast. Visibility was bad, skies had been overcast and no celestial sights were possible. To complicate matters neither R/DF nor echo-sounding was available.

I had been keeping a meticulous line of estimated positions since leaving the Fastnet Rock. We passed the Scillies and Bishop Rock without seeing either. John then became very edgy about our position and the coming landfall, so vital to the outcome of the race. Leaning over the chart he said, 'I have heard of yachts getting lost and going up the Bristol Channel instead of the English Channel.' 'Well, John,' I replied, 'I have just taken a fix by crossing the course of a butterfly which must have blown downwind from the flower gardens at St

Mary's in the Scillies, with the back-end view of a liner bound for the Great Circle course for New York. It exactly coincides with my estimated position!' Someone muttered that the butterfly might have originated in Africa and that the liner was probably going to Buenos Aires. John said drily, 'I still think that we might be going up the Bristol Channel.'

Later we crossed the finishing line at midnight, amid a *feu de joie* from the Plymouth Harbour defences, who happened to be carrying out practice firings that night, to discover somewhat to my surprise that we had won our class and also the Fastnet Challenge Cup for the overall winner – the ocean-racing equivalent of going into the winner's enclosure after the Grand National.

Many years later, I was bringing *Galway Blazer II* home from her solo circumnavigation into the Western Approaches to the English Channel. I had foolishly got myself a long way to the north of my intended mid-channel approach by dodging an area of bad weather to the southward.

By this date, 1972, radio direction-finding bearings of shore stations were available, and I obtained a fix from Round Island in the Scillies and Ushant off Brittany. Full of confidence I pressed on, reefed down in a half gale and in very poor visibility. Suddenly through the murk appeared a large vessel on a northerly course, obviously going between the Scillies and Land's End.

I realized in a flash, that I had got myself lost, that I had been in great danger of emulating Sir Cloudisley Shovell, whose squadron of sailing ships was wrecked on the rocks around the Scillies, but that at least I now knew where I was. The D/F bearing of Ushant had been distorted by 'bounce back' off the coast, a phenomenon with which I had not been familiar. Primarily I think the error was due to the fact that I had not been sufficiently thorough in maintaining my estimated position while dodging trawlers all night on the fishing banks.

REGULATIONS FOR PREVENTING COLLISIONS AT SEA

A few years ago, I decided to obtain Yachtmasters' Certificates, Ocean and Offshore. After some correspondence, it was decided in general that I could be awarded certificates on all the evidence of my voyages:

the books, journals, logs, celestial sight books and the tracks of my charts.

The Irish Yachting Association decided, however, quite rightly, that I should have to be examined on the 'Collision Regulations' which had recently been altered, and on the new system of buoyage for which the verbal shorthand is IALA.

Being set on getting the certificates and at an age when schooling does not come easily I decided to study my subjects with ferocious application. I read, reread, memorized and read them again. I studied various ancillary regulations and bought pop-up cards showing the lights and shapes required to be exhibited by all the various classes of vessels. I felt that I was getting a bit too clever for my own good when I found what appeared to me to be certain anomalies in the rules and was moved to point them out to high authorities, receiving dusty answers in reply.

The night before the examination my daughter, who is an artist, was giving an exhibition of her work in Dublin. Like many young people's functions, this ceremony was fuelled by plonk. The next morning I had a bad headache and the corners of my brain had stuck together. What, I wondered, do they put in that stuff? I had difficulty in finding the bus to the examination centre. The examiner greeted me and said, 'You don't look too good this morning' and I felt bound to agree.

So intensive, however, had been my studies that the answers to the searching and conscientious examiner welled up out of my subconscious mind. I passed with flying colours, and was awarded Yacht-masters' Ocean Certificate 001 and, believe it or not, Offshore Certificate 007. The moral is that a prospective mariner can and should get all these regulations off pat, at the same time realizing that hundreds of drivers of small craft which he will encounter will have little or no knowledge of them. The lone sailor must be even more sure of the subject; with no one to support him, there is little time available to bob down below and consult books and diagrams. Furthermore, if you leave the sea for the winter season or perhaps for much longer, your knowledge will become rusty and the regulations may be altered; so you must bone up on them before putting to sea afresh. The traffic separation zones and the regulations governing them must be closely studied: apart from the dangers of collision, infringement of the regulations can, in certain cases, involve you in swingeing fines. In general, the lone sailor should whenever possible avoid these focal points of shipping.

Conversely to all this, I remember sailing into New York harbour a few years ago. The separation zones are shaped like a truncated starfish and I was paying particular attention to the scene, working my way out of potential trouble. Sadly it transpired that the port seemed to be little used. The only vessel encountered was a tug towing a rubbish barge. We nosed up to one of the harbour finger piers where there were dockers standing around and asked for directions to the Customs and Immigration Centre. The only response was from one docker who took down his trousers, turned round, bent over and exhibited his arse. Circumstances do alter cases.

If you wish further to lift the veil of mystique which surrounds the navigation art, get a copy of *The Shell Guide to Yacht Navigation* (Faber and Faber) by Captain John Coote, Royal Navy, one of the most experienced and successful ocean-racing navigators. The book is comprehensive, authoritative and amusing, which means that you can come up for air – so important in a technical manual – reasonably priced, and a good reference book or bedside reading. There is a foreword by Robin Knox-Johnston, one of Britain's foremost mariners and lone sailors.

CHAPTER FIVE

A Star to Steer Her By

At about 2 a.m. on a pitch-black night our small family group were driving home from a party along the deserted roads of County Monaghan. Suddenly the engine stopped. I got out, opened the bonnet and peered into blackness. Someone trudged off to try to find a cottage and get a light, for we had no flashlamps. Suddenly I had one of those bright ideas. I unscrewed the driving mirror and borrowed someone's compact mirror. One mirror was used to reflect a headlight backwards, the other mirror directed the beam down into the engine. It was clear that an electrical connection had fallen away. In those days women wore hairpins and one of these was used to remake the connection. The happiest part of the story is that the adjacent cottager, with the warmheartedness which is usual in rural Ireland, was in no whit aggrieved to be woken, and cheerfully provided a light, by now unnecessary as the engine was running.

Many years later I was navigating a yacht from Ireland to New York. We had storm damage in mid-Atlantic; a guard-rail stanchion was badly strained, breaking the deck, and sea-water leaked on to the electrical fuseboard. The first thing to fail was the compass light. I remembered that Irish party and the motor repair. Two mirrors properly mounted and adjusted threw the glare from the stern light on to the compass. Finally the stern light gave out, as did all the electrical systems of the boat. For a time we steered by a star at the stemhead setting to the westward. The sky clouded over. Then I began to think; and about time too!

I remembered reading a scientific report on the dipolar reversal of the earth's magnetic field. About seven hundred thousand years ago, it read, the earth's polarity was reversed. The reversal previous to that was about one million two hundred years earlier and so on backwards in astronomical and geological time. Some scientists believe that another reversal may be due soon.

To determine the course of these overwhelming events we must first look at the operative factor of the earth's magnetic field. The apparent movement of the moon relative to the earth, caused by the latter's daily rotation, and causing the oceanic tidal wave is also thought to generate a tidal movement in the internal liquid magma relative to the earth's solid outer crust on which we perch. This movement, which includes large quantities of ferrous metal, produces a vast dynamo which magnetizes the earth's axis and gives a normally unfailing aid to the mariner, who, copying the ancient Chinese, carries a magnetic compass.

The trigger for the dipolar reversal of this field is a gigantic meteorite striking the earth. It makes a dimple in the ground about a hundred miles across and drags after itself a vast fireball. The shock and decelerating effect cause a reversal of the magma's tide and thus a reversal of the earth's polarity. Now you may feel that unless one happened to be underneath or in the proximity of the colliding meteorite, no great adverse effects would develop, one would simply reverse the compass card. Alas, it appears, the reversal may not be immediate. The new field seems to take a long time to regenerate: it may be up to a thousand years.

So if all this research were to be borne out in practice, we should be without magnetic compasses, not just for a few dark nights, but for our lifetime.

I thought back to the land adventure which I previously mentioned. I was caught in a blizzard alone on a mountaintop, 9,000-feet up in New Zealand. Visibility was down to a few feet and the compass card rendered inoperative by magnetic ore in the mountain. The problem was how to get back to safety avoiding the dangerous crags which abounded. Obviously the first measure was to backtrack one's footsteps in the snow. Finally the footsteps were obliterated in a violent hailstorm. The only option then left open to me was to gauge very carefully the direction of the true wind and maintain a course which kept that direction constant. One had, at the same time, to utter a prayer that the wind would not change. I have jug-handle ears and these make excellent wind sensors; when running downwind they are an insurance against gybing; as soon as the wind creeps into the leeward ear you know that you are running by the lee and must steer a little more to windward. I have known one of these crashing gybes to break a crosstree spreader in a mid-Atlantic gale; I was not steering at the time. Back on that mountain, I trimmed my ears to a wind which fortunately did not change.

Now to transfer the mountain situation to the seagoing problem. Unlike the wind on the glacier, any change in the true wind will show its footprints in the sea. A fresh train of ripples or waves will run across that which was caused by the true wind prior to the change.

Suddenly forced to steer on a dark night with no compass I realized that the skill of sensing the true wind and any change in it needs a good deal of practice; I regretted that our vane steering was out of action because, as well as releasing the helmsman from the tiller, the vane will steer a course relative to the wind and will make any change immediately apparent, for the change of course will set up a change of sound and movement. The established wave train resultant from the wind previous to the change will slap and rock you from a different direction. If you are alone and alert it will wake you from a sleep and you can then readjust your course.

But now one had to steer, think and feel. Think how helpless one would feel without the aid of compass, timepiece and sextant. I recalled reading an article describing the methods of the early Pacific navigators who did just that. They were described as voyaging from Tahiti to Hawaii, commencing by steering roughly north by stern bearings of the Southern Cross; across the Equator the Pole Star rose and gave them a good northern track. After a while the priestly navigator would produce a half coconut shell pierced with a latitudinal circlet of little holes: filled with water just leaking at all holes it gave them an artificial horizon and a level. An eye to one hole would perceive when the Pole Star kissed the rim of the coconut. The angle which this made was exactly calculated for the latitude of Hawaii. They knew that the islands were to the east of them, so all they had to do was to turn right and keep going, checking their latitude from time to time with their set piece 'sextant'. The landfall was simple: the islands are high and clouds hover over them.

These mariners were fortunate in that the seas which they traversed were mostly under clear skies; the sun shone by day, the stars twinkled at night. I also recalled seeing a fishing boat filled with refugees which crossed the Atlantic from the Canaries to the Caribbean in that situation. They also were without charts. All had been confiscated by the authorities to try to prevent such an escape. They had, however, constant sun and stars to direct them; but the landfall was a gamble. I began to wonder if I could take an altitude of the Pole Star using a protractor with extensions – very doubtful, just try it.

Many years later I discovered a book, *The Voyaging Stars* by David Lewis. He had already become my hero after I read the account of his Antarctic circuit in *Ice Bird*.

Dr Lewis had also researched in great detail the expertise and traditions of the great native Pacific navigators. His account is both instructive and very moving as a human document. The ancient navigators, whose descendants have preserved their skills, colonized the myriad islands spread over a vast area of ocean. There is no mention here of the half coconut sextant and I have since been told on good authority that this was a myth. It does, however, point one's mind at the problem of measuring the altitude of the Pole Star by primitive means. What is certain is that they acquired and memorized an exact knowledge of the relative positions of the principal stars and used them in two ways.

First, a star at the zenith of its arc passes right overhead above points on the earth whose latitude equals the star's celestial latitude.

Thus, if the navigator is sufficiently skilful to be able, in a lurching vessel, to judge when his selected star is right overhead, he will know his latitude. An island is known by its overhead star.

Second, the bearings from the navigator's starting point, of the rising and setting of known stars were noted and courses set for other islands, allowing, of course, for ocean currents. When stars were not visible they would steer by wind direction. Skills were also developed to assist landfalls by observation of reflected swells and other wave patterns, by the flight of birds and by one very arcane discovery: outwards from islands there radiated phosphorescent streaks, about a fathom below the surface. Now what, I wonder, was this? Could it be underwater tracks of the emanations which activate extra-sensory perception? All this is very easy to write down, but to do it you need a lot of practice and dedication.

Further on in time I read an article in an American magazine called *Ocean Navigator* about someone who had a similar experience with a failed compass light. Furthermore, anything I can do he can do better, and did, so I hereby pay tribute to a really great navigator, Marvin Creamer.

In earlier voyages, before he denied himself the luxury of a compass, Creamer apparently had the same trouble as I did with a failed compass light. My only one-upmanship was my use of two mirrors to deflect the stern light into the compass; after that Marvin roars ahead. After coming to the same conclusions as I did about steering by wind direction and wave patterns, he decided to investigate total no-instrument oceanic sailing; after some transatlantic experiments he actually sailed around the world via the Southern Ocean without compass, timepiece other than an hourglass, or sextant, let alone any press-button gadgetry. All this was kept sealed in case of total loss of confidence and position. The chief points he has made are:

1   Steering, much as I have described.
2   Latitude estimation drawing from Dr Lewis by discovering which
      star is, during its meridian transit at the zenith (that is right
      overhead) in the latitude which you wish to attain. The
      judgement, from a moving platform, of when a star is right
      overhead, at first appears to me to be baffling – none the less
      with practice it was achieved.
3   Longitude can, of course, only be estimated from course and
      speed made good. This can be liable to errors if the ocean
      currents are misapplied, and landfalls were made by noting the
      greening of water on crossing the continental shelf and types
      of fish and birds encountered as land was closed. In this
      connection, I noticed that if you look at the map of the world
      the continents hang down fairly vertically and present their coasts
      to a large extent in longitudinal directions.

Thus, if you run along the latitude of your destination, you will make many landfalls with fair certainty. One of the exceptions is Australia, a large squarish box, and this is where Creamer seems to have had problems. Coming from South Africa to make a landfall on Tasmania he turned north to make his sighting, to discover the longitude was a thousand miles in error and met instead the western part of South Australia. I suppose that the ocean current had been applied wrongly. The intrepid navigator was, however, undeterred and continued his voyage, successfully making his other landfalls correctly.

Personally, I am lost in admiration for Creamer and his crew. I found it was wearing to steer by the wind and cannot conceive how endurance can be conjured up to achieve such a feat.

I suppose that in a no-instrument voyage you should not have vane steering.

I do not intend to emulate Lewis, Creamer or the Pacific navigators, but there are lessons here for the long-distance solo navigator:

1 Mind your compass and have a phosphorescent compass light.
2 Have a spare compass.
3 If, owing to accident, you are without a compass, or indeed any other manufactured aids to navigation, you need not despair; there is a star to steer her by.
4 One should, however, put some research and practice into this last.

CHAPTER SIX

The Bermuda Triangle

Bermuda has given its name to a well-known item of one's holiday wardrobe, Bermuda shorts, and I remember someone, a trifle confused, who thought that the Bermuda Triangle was an article of abbreviated female swimwear. But no, it is a triangular stretch of water whose corners are Bermuda, the Florida Keys and the Leeward Islands. One side includes the most malignant part of the Gulf Stream, from Cape Hatteras in North Carolina to the Bahamas.

Within this stretch of water, it is thought, lurks some vast sinister esoteric force: perhaps a giant Kraken whose huge tentacles can reach up and drag vessels down to their doom, can even reach up and pick aircraft out of the sky. Or is there perhaps some vortex creating a hole in the sea with a hole in the atmosphere above it? Yes, I am afraid that this sort of nonsense is widely believed. At any rate, it provides a ready-made alibi for navigators.

Competing in the Bermuda Race of 1950 in *Galway Blazer*, I approached Bermuda from the north in high excitement. Our class was the smallest in the race; in fact we had only been let in on special sufferance. I had a splendid crew of young experts and from reports on the radio we seemed to be doing well. I kept a constant line of positions from astronomical sights and exactly gauged the west-going current. As we got closer to the reefs which are about 15 miles north of the Island, the skies clouded over; no more sights were possible.

I had on board a new gadget, a radio direction-finding W/T set, and I started to take bearings of a beacon on the island. From these bearings it appeared that the current had eased off, so I altered course directly for where the buoy should have been at the end of the reefs. Suddenly we saw a buoy, not ahead as we had hoped, but way off to the eastward and upwind. Simultaneously, I realized that we should have a longish beat up to it, which cost us third place in our class, that we were heading for the reefs, that the D/F bearings had been faulty (actually it was a fixed set and subject to heeling error), and that our original course would have been correct. Further, I reread the sailing directions which announced that to that date 1,500 ships have been wrecked on the reefs around Bermuda: not a Kraken, just a small low island where visibility is frequently poor and reefs extend far out to sea. In fact the whole edifice is the crater of a vast submerged extinct volcano.

Many years later I was sailing up towards Bermuda from southward. We made a good landfall but visibility was again poor and it was hard to identify the landmarks. Finally, I got three bearings of known objects, but the resultant plotted fix gave a large cocked-hat which was shaming until I looked again at the chart and noticed the warning, 'Magnetic anomalies in this area'. I remembered my experience on the volcano in New Zealand when my compass pointed down towards the ferrous core. We arrived in harbour to find that Hurricane Alberto had fizzed north of the island; two yachts were rolled over with loss of life, one was struck by lightning and the Bermuda Race postponed for two days.

Fortunately, the whale which had hit us off Portugal (see Chapt.7) caused enough damage to delay us long enough to postpone our arrival in the Gulf Stream until after the hurricane had passed.

In our subsequent voyage northward to Newport, Rhode Island, we had to cross the Gulf Stream, a notorious breeding-ground of storms and squalls owing to the unstable atmospheric conditions caused by the proximity of warm water and air over the Gulf Stream and cold water and air coming down on the Greenland Current. We met one sudden line squall which threatened to take the rig off, though we ran before it, but the most sinister happening for me was to discover that we had been set backwards for 72 miles in the twenty-four hours. This represents 3 knots. I read in the sailing directions that the Gulf Stream gives off meanders, sometimes as much as 3 knots in any direction. I had scarcely believed this and thought it was reported by someone who had made a mess of the navigation or who wanted an excuse for losing the Bermuda Race; but I was then certain of my sights and I had a check from another reliable sight-taker.

Back again to the Bermuda Race in 1950. I was sailing north from

Bermuda to New York to refit for the race. There was a frightful storm which battered other yachts sailing the same track, but fortunately I had sailed earlier and got across the worst of the storm area before it erupted. A strong north-easterly wind then blew down from the Newfoundland Banks bringing the typical weather of that area, thick fog: a nasty experience in a focal point for shipping and for making a landfall on Long Island for which I had not been able to obtain tidal information. Combination of all these experiences with the known meteorological facts of the proximity of the Atlantic Polar Front, which separates either continental polar air of North America from marine tropical air of the North Atlantic or marine polar air of the North Atlantic from marine tropical air of the North Atlantic, must indicate an area of potential instability. Furthermore, Cape Hatteras sticks out into the Gulf Stream at its strongest and makes a classic, weather turning-point. All this adds to the fact that the Bermuda Triangle and its northern offshoot, the Gulf Stream, is not the abode of some demonic force field but a place where a great many natural hazards happen to lurk.

I am reminded of Agamemnon the Greek commander-in-chief whose fleet was weather-bound in the Aegean on its voyage to attack Troy. The King sacrificed his daughter, Iphigenia, took her ashore and cut her throat. The gods were apparently satisfied and the weather moderated, but I think he would have been better advised to have consulted the local fisherman about the Aegean weather pattern.

So the lone sailor should eschew the idea that there are arcane forces at work in the Bermuda Triangle, for this will be confusing. What is required is to realize the various hazards and pay the requisite attention to seamanship, navigation and meteorology. Between ourselves, I should give the whole area a miss.

CHAPTER SEVEN

Disasters

The ultimate disaster is perhaps when you are alone, a long way offshore and a hole appears in the bottom of your boat through which you can see blue water. It is, I think, sufficiently important for me to give you a blow-by-blow account of this very occurrence.

I departed from Fremantle, Western Australia, on 12 December 1971 with the intention of sailing south of Tasmania, Stewart Island, the southernmost part of New Zealand, Cape Horn and non-stop to Plymouth, Devon. As usual at that time of year I had to beat out against a sou'wester and finally made an offing to clear Cape Leeuwin, the south end of Western Australia. The wind then backed to south and I was free to point for south of Stewart Island, off Otago, New Zealand. It blew a good Force 5, all plain sail was set and a feeling of immense euphoria lightened my heart.

At about 1600, I was down below, doing some chore just forward of the mainmast and facing to port. Suddenly there was an awful bang: the boat shuddered and under my horrified gaze a giant carbuncle mushroomed inwards on the boat's hull. It was 2 or 3 feet across. There were splits, rents and cracks across it, water was gushing into the boat. As the damage extended to below the waterline and it was on the lee side, we were sitting on top of it and it was well pressed down. One of the ribs across it which had previously been concave was now convex. It just held, but only just.

Panic! I raced up on deck with all the alternative causes racing through my brain. Navigation had perhaps gone haywire and we had hit Australia supposedly hundreds of miles away; although I had recently been on deck, had I failed to notice another vessel? Wreckage was a strong possibility. An iceberg was marked on the chart as having been recorded here in some bygone age. Killer whales were known to have abounded in the days of the South Australian whale fishery, preying on the unfortunate hunted sperm whales and actually aiding their human tormentors, acting as auxiliary drivers of the prey; finally the great white shark, another relentless killer, is known to inhabit these waters.

There was nothing in sight on the surface of the sea, a grey-green swirl was disappearing in my wake.

Many years previously, I was sailing a 30sq metre, *Tre Sang*, from moorings in the Clyde where she had lain all summer, for Gosport. We ran into a southerly buster in the Estuary and it transpired that planks had opened up in the sun and on one tack the water poured in. It did not take long to twig the fact that one must get on the other tack, allow the wind to press the boat over and lift the crack out of the water and then make a rough job caulking the leak. I had then two crew members with me and, although seasick, they were at that time able to help.

Out in the Southern Ocean, however, I suspect that panic had clouded my mind and, if it had not been for a memory of that incident in the Clyde, I might not have made the quick and obvious decision to put the boat on the other tack, then alas pointing for Antarctica, and lift the damage upwards. Now the water was only splashing in from waves, the spouting had stopped.

I pumped out the water in the bilges and made a craven rush for my radio transmitter. 'Mayday' went out in hysterical yelps. A terrible feeling of guilt at calling out the rescue services swept over me, partly assuaged, I confess, by the fact that I was a personal friend of the senior naval officer in Fremantle. All this was a glorious waste of time. There was a defect in the transmitter: no signal got through. This did wonderfully concentrate my mind. I had at first thought out the alternatives: one, go gurgling down with the boat; two, get in my one-man inflatable life-raft and survive perhaps hours or days; or three, jump over the side and get it over.

Despair had set in as panic subsided. However, the boat was afloat; on the new tack the leak was containable. It was now up to me, someone I had never thought very much of, but who now, for a change, got it right.

I realized that repairs could be made and that they must be made quickly. If the wind subsided we should come upright, the damage

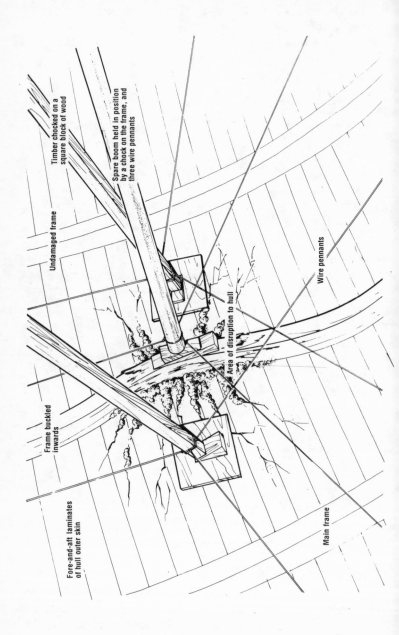

Timber chocked on a square block of wood

Spare boom held in position by a chock on the frame, and three wire pennants

Undamaged frame

Wire pennants

Area of disruption to hull

Frame buckled inwards

Fore-and-aft laminates of hull outer skin

Main frame

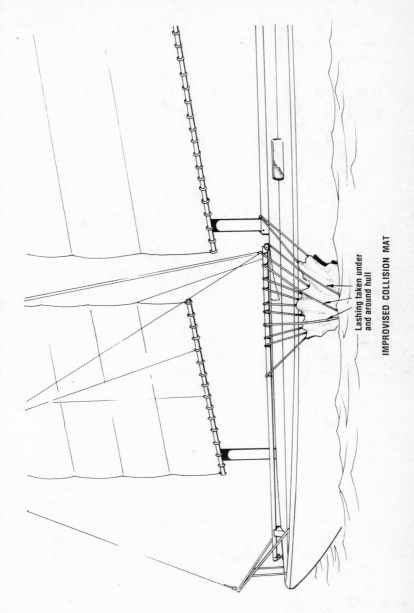

Lashing taken under
and around hull

IMPROVISED COLLISION MAT

Above and opposite Repairs after being holed by a Great White Shark, south
of Australia.

would no longer be lifted out of the water and the leaks would no longer be containable; if it blew strongly the situation would probably become out of hand.

All through the long period of frenzied endeavour I raced between repair work and the pump. The first thing I tried was according to classic instruction. I should secure a sail over the damaged area on the outside. This ploy often works when the topsides of a boat are stove in. However, I doubted if sailcloth would be effective in rough seas below the waterline. Leaving the pumps for fifteen-minute intervals I dragged the storm jib up on deck and prepared it with fore-and-aft lines, a lowering line and a bottom line. It took hours, but by degrees I hove the sail down taut over the damage and slipped below to inspect the effect which it had. To my dismay the sail, being too big and clumsy to adapt itself to the wineglass hull, was acting as a water-scoop and vastly increasing the inflow. Laboriously I gathered the jib in and stowed the soggy mass below. Possibly it might have worked if we came to a stop, but this I dared not risk; the hole had to be raised above sea level.

The first thing I had to do was to plug the worst of the rents and cracks. I used a combination of the towelling which I had used to keep the spray and rain from getting down my neck, combined with strips of sponge rubber which I had on board by pure chance.

All this had to be done with delicacy to avoid enlarging the damage. About every fifteen minutes I had to break off to pump the bilges. As my repairs improved the situation, the intervals between pumping became mercifully and progressively longer. My main fear was that the bent rib would give way, and I next attended to this.

I had a spare main boom and I cut this off to a suitable length to make a shore. The inner end bore up against a strength piece on the hull opposite to the damage. The end bearing on the rib I first positioned by lengths of rope tightened in three opposing directions; then I hammered in hard wood wedges to make a firm support.

I next tackled the outside of the hull. I inspected the damage with a sinking heart – it looked appalling. My idea was to nail something over the damage, preferably a square of canvas. I hung myself upside down over the side by my heels and started to hammer long, boat-builders' saw-nails into the hard mahogany. It was a failure: I could not hammer them in straight in the existing conditions. On my subsequent voyage I took shorter, broad-headed tack nails; now they were six hundred miles away; water was pouring up my nose to discourage me further.

I then remembered from my old battleship days 'the collision mat'. This was an article for damage control, to cover a hole in the hull caused by an enemy torpedo.

It consisted of a large square mat, about 20 feet across with eyelets at each corner. It was made of canvas with oakum worked into it so that one side of it looked like a tatty fur coat. A chain bottom-line was kept permanently rigged and this was attached to the lowest corner of the mat; a lowering line opposite to this was manned by a group of strong Royal Marines. Their buddies then hauled away on the bottom line on the other side of the ship. The remaining corners were attached to lines leading well forward and aft and manned by seamen. The Royal Marine tug-of-war team hauled so strongly that they almost lifted the battleship out of the water. With the fore-and-afters taut the oakum 'thrums' made a watertight compress. Meanwhile, the shipwrights below would be shoring up bulkheads and trying to isolate the damage.

So I decided to make a collision mat. The bottom-line had to be passed by sitting up in the bows, throwing the loop of a line over the stem and paying both ends out as I wriggled aft on my bottom. I had two partial failures with first a square piece of canvas locker-top, then a pair of mackintosh trousers, too small. I did, however, improve them by passing more lines under the boat and hauling them taut on top of the mats to clamp them. But square sides don't fit on a curved surface and wineglass hull form. The battleships had been slab-sided.

Suddenly I thought of a long-past lesson in applied mechanics: a four-legged chair with one short leg will rock, a three-legged chair cannot. In a burst of light I visualized a triangular mat. Working at fevered pace I unpicked the triangular strengthened tackpiece of the storm jib which I had previously used as a jury sail. It was easy to fit, had an eyelet at one corner and sail tapes, which could be knotted, up the sides. In place, hauled taut and clamped down with two more ropes over it, the trick was done. I foresaw that I should soon dare to sail on the other tack with the damage underneath me.

Some very tricky fine work had then to be done. I worked some sticky tape impregnated with yellow goo (mercury chromate) into all the remaining fine cracks and then made three timber pads to cover the weakest parts of the carbuncle of cracked wood. These were held in place by three more shores positioned like the shore on the rib, but lightly wedged with soft wood to avoid splintering off the damaged portion. All this took three days, during which I was sailing in the wrong direction. Mercifully the wind stayed as it was, pressing the boat over, keeping the damage high and relatively dry.

Sometimes I would rest, getting up to pump as necessary – but not much rest.

At last I had the confidence to tack and head for Fremantle. The pace was slow, the thirteen ropes round the hull acted as a brake and made a drumming noise in the water. The repairs held and I sailed home thankfully.

I had the boat hauled out in a yard for fishing boats, run by a man of Yugoslav origins called Marko. He was one of the strongest men I have ever seen and one of the kindest. I appreciated how right I had been to treat the splintered wood with such care and respect when Marko, using no tools, ripped off the damaged portions with his bare hands. For once, I felt, I *had* got it right.

I assumed that the most likely identity of my attacker was the Great White Shark (*Carcarias carcarias* is its Latin name and it is descended from an extinct species, *Carcarias carcaradon* which grew to 96 feet!)

Not wishing to repeat this performance, I did a great deal of research on the characteristics of sharks. I discovered the fact that they are not colour blind and are sensitive to contrasting colours. Observing that red is the colour of blood, flesh and wounded prey and that white is the colour of the bellies of many sea creatures, I came to the conclusion that these colours were just what one did not need to display. My boat's bottom had been red and the sides were white. These I altered to sea green and sky blue. I wished that I had done this research earlier, but I had no further trouble of this nature on my subsequent voyage around Cape Horn and back to Plymouth. Many years later, however, I was asked to sail a boat across the Atlantic for someone else. I noticed that the bottom was white. I urged the owner to repaint it blue: at the time the expense seemed forbidding and I was not sufficiently pressing.

We sailed white-bottomed and were rammed off Portugal by a

whale. Fortunately, on this occasion the damage was not very severe and I had a strong crew.

I think the probability is that killer whales or great white sharks may attack a boat mistaking it for their normal prey, including the larger whales which feed on krill and plankton. I believe that these latter would not normally be aggressive towards one's boat, but may well mistake it for some fellow creature and like cattle in a field come up to give it a friendly barge, resulting sometimes in unintended catastrophe. I have become a strong believer in colour camouflage, though I am bound to admit that some experts disagree with me. However, if you take an action in which you firmly believe, it does give you a certain peace of mind, perhaps akin to the old-fashioned doctor's placebo, the bread pill, which cured the patient by calming his brain.

The lesson I have learned from a lot of seagoing experience is that one should spend a considerable time in quiet thought contemplating the main disasters which may occur and visualizing the methods which could be employed to rectify them and the equipment required for repairs, within the limitations of available stowage. The main obvious disasters are:

1 Hull damage
2 Mast damage
3 Sail damage, including deterioration due to prolonged exposure to ultra-violet rays in strong sunlight
4 Rudder damage
5 Damage to standing rigging and chafed running rigging
6 Last and most important, damage to oneself. This I shall deal with in Chapter 11, on self-preservation.

I shall pass briefly over disaster damage to masts, sails and rigging. Recovery from these depends on foresight and provision of the necessary spare parts and repair gear which I shall discuss later (Chapter 11) and your own skill as a shipwright, sailmaker and rigger which should be practised and developed; and finally, of course, your own ingenuity and endurance in measuring up to the circumstances.

I considered at one time that my experience of being holed below the water line was the ultimate disaster and so it then seemed. But not really. The ultimate disaster may be damage to yourself. For then you have no one else to call on and may be incapacitated from dealing with emergencies or even perhaps from the simple handling of the boat.

The following personal experience, seeming at first to be trivial, might well have expanded into disaster. I recount it, partly because the outcome might be useful to anyone caught in a like situation, afloat or even ashore, and to concentrate the mind on the vulnerability of the body of the lone sailor.

I was sailing eastwards about two hundred miles south of the Cape of Good Hope in surprisingly nice weather. I had observed that there was some chafe aloft in the rigging and that it would be necessary to get myself up the mast. I went below to assemble some equipment and then, I suspect, made an unnecessarily hurried dash through the hatch to gain the deck, passing through at speed and in a bent and cramped posture.

An agonizing pain shot through my spine. To use a layman's term, my back had locked. I could move only with pain and difficulty. It did not seem fair (Murphy's Fourth Law) as I do not have what is popularly called 'a back'.

It was now obvious that I could not get up the mast, continue with my voyage or, if bad weather or other difficulties arose, handle the situation. I decided to turn northward and seek a port in South Africa, hoping that conditions would remain tolerable. I crawled below and went to the chart table to make an intensive study of the charts, sailing directions and pilot charts of the area and to select my courses and port of refuge.

Now this is important. I stood at the chart table with legs apart and still, back hollow and bottom in the air, elbows on the chart table, totally immobilized against the movement of the boat. I held this position for a very long time, probably between one and two hours, in order to memorize the details of what looked like a hairy passage to safety. Finally, with a sigh I rose to implement my intentions. My back was free and painless. Subsequently I recounted this event to someone versed in orthopaedic surgery who remarked, 'Well, you happened to do the right thing'. I never succeeded in persuading my friends, stricken by back trouble in normal life, to try my 'cure'; but it impressed upon me very forcibly the urgent necessity of looking after oneself, as did another occasion when I neglected to obey the simple rule – don't fall over the side – so important when you are alone.

The boat lay becalmed in the Doldrums and I took advantage of the inactivity to do some experiments with the rigging of the foresail, pushing out the boom while overhauling the sheet. I was not hooked on and had no guard rails, relying on my agility and balance to counter the movement of the boat in the swells. Then came an unexpected lurch, the foresail boom ran out and I dived over the side. Normally, if I had to go into the sea, say to scrub off goose barnacles, I should have a lifeline on me and hang a bowline over the side to climb up the very high freeboard of my boat.

Now I visualized a sudden puff of wind sailing the boat away or my rather feeble arms unavailingly pulling up the side over the tumblehome of the hull, while perhaps a shark snapped at my toes. I swam fast back to the boat and, with a terrific impetus from a leg stroke, just got my fingers over the toerail; then ensued a few unavailing tugs and the muscles of my 'mighty' arms stood out like sparrows' kneecaps.

Then I remembered the modern high-jumper's roll over, threw my head and shoulders and one arm sideways and downwards, kicked my pelvis and legs up and got one foot over the toerail. The rest was easy except for some scratches from barnacles. I regained the deck and simultaneously appreciated that there were in fact no sharks around and it would have been far easier to scramble over the stern where the freeboard was less and where the vane gear would have been an aid.

'OH DEAR, MY RUDDER HAS GONE!'

Only once in my yachting career has my steering failed. This was in a yacht which I will not identify for fear of court action through Messrs Sue, Grabbitt and Runne. In this yacht the steering quadrant was held to the rudder-stock by a friction block. There was no positive attachment nor anything to prevent it from dropping off the spline if the screws of the friction block slacked off through vibration; and this is what happened. The quadrant dropped down and fouled in the bolts of the rudder-stock stuffing box and gland. By an unbelievable stroke of good fortune this occurred in harbour; not at sea, at night in a gale on a lee shore. Even so it was very difficult to repair the gear, which was awkward to get at unless you had a midget in the crew.

This sort of incident encourages one to give thought to the action which should be taken in case of the failure of the steering gear at sea and should impel one to try out these measures in a practice run. Why, I wonder, is there never time for this?

What should be done must depend on the circumstances and the equipment and skills which are available, and rather than lay down rules I shall give some general suggestions.

Fabricated rudder or steering oar   This is extremely difficult to make if you are not a skilled carpenter. A door on a spar is a classic solution. One might copy the Pacific canoe voyagers and construct a simple, lowering steering board: lowering will put the centre of effort aft, and the bow should come up to windward. Raising the board has the opposite effect. If you carry a sweep or yulow it could be a help, perhaps not as a primary rudder but to pull you round on course and to get under way with other methods to follow.

Towed substitute rudder   This might be an anchor or some fabricated drogue. I have read that the trick is to tow it over one quarter and rig a line from it to the other quarter. If you tow it from dead centre there is not enough leverage on either line to the quarters, but I wonder if one had a strong spar across the counter with ropes for the drogue to blocks on the ends and lead into a whipstaff, might it work? Let's try it.

Steering with the sails   Steering with the sails is, I think, the best bet, and in any case could be backed up by the other methods.

(a)   Close hauled and reaching. There is, of course, the well-known method of trimming the sails to 'fight' one another. The mainsail is sheeted a little slacker than normal, the jib well trimmed. If the boat takes a sheer to windward the mainsail will lose power and the jib will press her back on course. If the boat steers to windward the jib will become inefficient, the mainsail gains power and steers her back. If you have a mizzen there is another force with which to play.

(b)   Downwind is more difficult. The downwind steering for single-handers, invented I think by Marin Marie, consisted of twin

1. Oranmore Castle, County Galway.

2. Bobby Somerset. One of the founding
fathers of modern ocean racing.

3. Blondie Hasler in 1953.

5. Bill King with his family before setting forth: son Tarka, wife Anita Leslie,
and daughter Leonie.

4. The bare hull of *Galway Blazer II* nearing completion at Souter's yard in Cowes. Designer Angus Primrose on the left. Builder Wilf Souter at right.

6. *Galway Blazer II*'s sailing trials off Cowes with fully battened junk rig.

7. Inspiration for the sail plan pioneered by Blondie Hasler in his junk-rigged Folkboat *Jester*, here shown with her subsequent owner, Mike Richey.

8. Exchanging good wishes with Nigel Tetley at Plymouth after the first single-handed Round the World Race. Tetley in his trimaran *Victress* was rescued after capsizing within reach of the finish.

9. Francis Chichester by his self-steering gear in *Gipsy Moth III*, winner of the first single-handed Transatlantic Race – for a wager of 20 pence.

10. Robin Knox-Johnston in his traditional double-ender *Suhaili*,
the first man to circumnavigate the globe non-stop
from point to point.

11. Alain Colas in a typical high-technology French multihull, *Manureva* (ex *Pen Duick*). Lost at sea.

12. A new frontier to conquer. Bill King, aged seventy-eight, making his first hang-gliding flight from a 8,000-foot peak in the French Alps.

foresails boomed out either side on whisker poles heeled just by the mainmast, topped up clear of the waves and canted forward about 20° before each beam with foreguys. It was used by the author in 1949 to cross the Atlantic in *Galway Blazer*. We never had to steer from the Canaries to Antigua; but it required a rudder, the jibs were sheeted to the tiller and, when a sheer took place, increased pressure on the windward jib and pulled the tiller to correct the course. However, I think that if the rudder was not available, careful adjustment of the sheets might mean that the jibs steered the boat by themselves.

JUNK RIG

This brings me to the single-hander's dilemma if the vane steering becomes unavailable. Some people seem to be able to steer for months: as far as I am concerned a few hours is enough. I said to myself, 'The vane steering *must* work.' I felt that I should never get the junk rig to steer itself, I could not lead sheets to the tiller which was below the deck. In the event this line of thought encouraged me to carry sufficient spares and to maintain the excellent gear with a fanatical degree of conscientiousness. It never broke down. On my return voyage up the Atlantic I passed to leeward of the Cape Verde Islands through the track of the Sargassum Weed. This seaweed detaches from the rocks around the Cape Verdes where the trade winds blow strongly and travels on the trade wind current to the Sargasso Sea in the centre of the vortex of the North Atlantic circulation of currents.

It has learned to live floating free and must, I suppose, feed on plankton; it has a complete family of sea creatures living on it, mostly disguised as seaweed, and it piles up in the vortex. I have long ago sailed nervously through it, patches like large hayfields appear and one looks for leads between them. But on this recent occasion, the weed started to wrap around the steering blade of the vane gear until it became like a club and lost power: the boat spun round in circles. I sat gloomily on the quarter, pushing the weed off with a boathook and thinking negative thoughts. After a while I discovered that I could make the Chinese rig sail itself without rudder, steering on any point of sailing, the boomed, fully-battened foresail being a tremendous advantage. With a following wind, the trick is, of course, to have the foresail trimmed in somewhat, the mainsail being slacked away nearly abeam; if the boat steers to windward the foresail gains power and the mainsail starts to weather-cock. Back she comes: with a sheer to leeward the mainsail gains power, and the foresail, being over-trimmed, is ineffective; hey presto! Now I wonder if in a white man's boat one could do something similar using a boomed-out jib; more difficult, I guess.

OTHER RUDDERS

Galway Blazer II had a normal skeg rudder. Having a belt and braces mentality I had a spare rudder constructed with pintles; gudgeons were fitted on the counter and drop-nosed pins kept the gudgeons secure on the pintles. I tried shipping it in place in harbour. I could just do it, but wondered if it needed a stronger man to ship it in a seaway.

It was never required and, weighing about a hundredweight, it compared unfavourably with the fabled drilled toothbrush handles in *Myth of Malham*.

I noticed that the Hydrovane steering gear, which I should choose if I ever owned a boat again, had the steering blade fitted so that in the event of failure of primary steering it could be used as an auxiliary rudder.

To sum up all this: one should give this matter a great deal of thought in relation to the type of boat which you sail and take time off to do some experiments. Do not be like me and wait until you are in a jam.

These accounts of some disasters are intended to alert your mind to various risks. In the next chapter I intend to make suggestions about how to look after yourself generally and what sorts of equipment to carry when you are a long way from ship chandlers or medical assistance.

'DON'T GO NEAR THE LAND!'

The Cruel Sea was the title of a gripping wartime novel by Nicholas Monsarrat, from which was made a very moving film starring Trevor Howard, an actor of immense authority. Personally I never feel safe when lone sailing until I am 500 miles offshore. I calculate that in this situation any prolonged storm would have blown itself out before drifting me on to a lee shore at the mercy of the cruel land.

Vessels do founder in mid-ocean, but by far the greatest number of shipwrecks occur along the coasts and on the edges of shoal water. At the point where turbulence at the base of the wave feels the sea bottom, the shape of the wave, which in deep water in the case of a simple single wave train is a gentle sine curve, becomes increasingly steeper. Apart from the tendency of the sea to form crests to break, a small vessel can fall down the front of a wave and be tripped over by the drag of its keel.

There is a government publication called *Meteorology for Mariners* (MET. 0.985 (1978)) which says on page 44:

When a deep water wave enters shallow water it undergoes profound modification. Its speed is reduced, the direction of motion may be changed and finally its height increases until, on reaching a certain limiting depth the wave breaks on the shore. Water may be regarded as shallow where the depth is less than half the length of the wave.

On page 39 there is a table (3.3) of wave lengths and speed in terms of period which tabulates wave lengths to a maximum of 624 metres. This is getting on for 700 yards and one begins to appreciate the old sailors' tales of Cape Horn greybeards measuring half a mile from crest to crest.

Without exaggeration, however, it stems from all this that 'shallowness' may begin to be felt at a depth of approximately 340 yards which is 170 fathoms and includes the edge of the continental shelf.

And this brings me to my point because I believe this to be a place of danger in very heavy weather. I have read, and regret that I do not have to hand, accounts of large vessels being broken up in heavy weather on the edge of the continental shelf off the coast of East Africa. Also I read a horrifying account of a friend, Mike Richey, whose junk-rigged folkboat *Jester* was capsized in a storm right on the edge of the continental shelf west of Ireland. In both these areas there are definite ocean currents and I wonder in my unscientific way if there may not be an up-welling there of water which may add to the turbulence and the possibility of the waves feeling the bottom. Other factors which might be possibilities are the storm surge, the pile-up of water ahead of very high winds and the raising of the tidal wave in an area of very low pressure. Certainly most mariners recognize the dangers on the edges of shoal water.

The report of the Institute of Oceanographic Sciences on severe wave conditions during the disastrous Fastnet Race in August 1979 discounts the fact that the yachts which suffered most in that disaster were near the Labadie Bank as being a contributory cause to their disaster. Oceanographers must know their job, also they had the evidence of the crews of the yachts as to the wave length of the seas running at the time, difficult though this may be to estimate when more than one wave train is running, but still I cannot help maintaining some heretical feelings.

The report cites the wave period during the most severe winds as being up to 12 seconds, and the table quoted above gives the wave length for this period as 250 yards; halve this for the depth when the waves 'feel' the sea-bed and are significantly altered by it, which comes to 120 yards, or 60 fathoms. The mean depth in the area where most of the 1979 Fastnet casualties occurred was 55 fathoms.

Now let us assume that I am wrong and the report is correct in its assumptions, as well it may be. None the less I am convinced that the lone sailor, who is particularly vulnerable, should if possible avoid the edges of any shoal water at the onset of very heavy weather. Very difficult to achieve, you may well say, but steps in this direction can be taken if you try to avoid banks for another reason – for here is where the fishermen abound. They are very much a law unto themselves as you have to give way to them while they are fishing. This is sometimes difficult as they frequently make sudden unheralded alterations of course and speed and their bright deck-lights keep them night-blind to small vessel lights; also like lorries on the motorway they are usually bigger than you are.

CHAPTER EIGHT

Very Heavy Weather

'Oh let us never never doubt, what nobody is sure about.'
Hilaire Belloc

If you wish to study this subject in depth I recommend *Heavy Weather Sailing* by Adlard Coles, a definitive and well-illustrated book: people often tell me that the illustrations terrify them.

I set out here to analyse the subject and apply the different aspects of the problem to the various kinds of boat which sail the ocean. I believe that the design, scantlings and rig of your boat should largely dictate your course of action.

Studying the accounts of two very great lone sailors I noticed that Robin Knox-Johnston in *Suhaili* attributed his survival when running downwind in Southern Ocean storms to his action of trailing warps astern to steady the boat and break the seas before they reached him. Bernard Moitessier, however, attributed his survival to having cut loose his warps, which he felt were endangering him, perhaps by keeping the boat partly sea-anchored to a piece of water other than that which was acting upon her; in other words not allowing the boat to roll with the punches. Two very great experts appear to disagree, and this, of course, happens in many other fields of human endeavour, all of which may simply be variations on a theme.

To go back to first principles, let us ask ourselves what are the principal dangers posed by heavy weather offshore. These are:

1 Big seas sweeping the decks and carrying away, or damaging, deck houses, rig or yourself.
2 The waterfalling effect of a body of water in a breaking wave falling on top of the boat and smashing the deck or tophamper.

51

This happened to Humphrey Barton in his tiny *Vertue XXXV* whilst riding to a sea-anchor in a storm north of Bermuda in 1950, and doubtless to many others.

3 Pitchpoling, that is the boat turning upside down end-over-end. This may occur when running down-wind and coming down off the front of a wave when the bow buries itself with the momentum of the boat accelerating at a steep angle and the stern is lifted before the crest breaks. This is potentially the most destructive accident of all. Miles Smeeton in *Tzu Hang*, together with his wife Beryl and crew member John Guzzwell, experienced this in the Southern Ocean. Their recovery, patching up of the wreckage of their boat and rig and subsequent voyage to safety is one of the great sagas of sea voyaging.

4 Capsizing or rolling over sideways. This mostly happens when a boat is more or less beam on to the sea and falls down the front of a steep wave. The keel 'catching' in the water sets up a capsizing moment, aided by the pressure of wind and water in the rig, and over she goes. My own experience is of this happening together with a half pitchpole while upside down.

Now for my own conclusions on all this, based on experience, intuition and reading, but supported by little scientific knowledge:

Design of the boat   I suppose that the most indestructible craft would be a log of wood with a hollowed-out capsule in the middle into which the pilot would insert himself like a termite; propulsive arrangement might be difficult, perhaps he would have to drift. The seas could not harm him.

I remember going aboard *Suhaili* when she was hauled out ashore and thinking that with her immensely strong construction she was the nearest thing to the indestructible log; furthermore, I thought that she was fortunate in having an indestructible human being on board. I remember meeting Robin at a party at the Polish Embassy in London. During discussion over some excellent Polish vodka I put a hand on his arm to discover myself clutching what appeared to be a 6-inch wire rope.

So why did Bernard Moitessier, an intelligent, witty and very experienced sailor, cut his warp loose? His boat *Joshua* was steel built and strong. Steel is non-buoyant and to make a very strong hull with positive buoyancy you need a large battleship. Bernard thought perhaps that those terrible waterfalls might crush his hull as one squeezes a sardine tin.

Now to revert to my own boat *Galway Blazer* and her design and construction.

1 She was of ultra-light build, 4½ tons, 30-foot water line, 42 feet overall, with four laminations of plywood cold-moulded and glued, total thickness ¾ inch with high freeboard. Her cockpit was below the deck and had two circular access hatches into which hurricane hatchcovers could be fitted, one of which had a plastic astrodome.

2 Her long overhung bow was spoon shaped and in this bulge was terrific buoyancy. She ran downwind in a hurricane all night. Each time she lifted her stern to race down the face of a wave into what looked like a bottomless pit, I felt by the seat of my pants that she must pitchpole. She did not: that bow saved her, I think. *Tzu Hang* had a narrow bow.

What else was so very good in her design? Her deck was whale backed and she had no deck houses, put up no obstruction to the heavy seas; she had no guard-rail stanchions to weaken the decksides. When I met Bernard in Plymouth he noticed my lack of guard rails and said, 'But Bill, you will spend most of your time in ze sea.' I showed him my safety lines, a wire running the length of the boat on either side of the mast. On to these I would hook my personal safety line and move up and down the deck like a tethered goat. He sagely nodded his approval.

Eventually, and *after* the hurricane subsided, my boat was rolled over and this is how it happened.

The general weather pattern in the area was vastly disturbed by an irruption of Antarctic air into Africa. The temperature in tropical or subtropical places dropped by staggering amounts: I read of a drop of 80°F and scarcely believed this; many tropical animals died of cold. A very vigorous depression must have passed fairly close south of us and the hurricane-force winds backed through 90° from NW to SW, causing two gigantic seas running across one another. Fishermen in Tristan da Cunha just north of me reported the worst weather in living memory. I ran downwind under bare poles successfully for about twelve hours and then realized I was becoming exhausted from steering.

I let the boat lie ahull, beam on to the wind and sea, with great trepidation. The junk rig, with the windage of the masts up forward, will not 'heave to' with the bow poking up to windward, the boat moving under windage of hull and masts, fore-reaching. She lay dead in the water, quite the most perilous position. None the less she rode it out while I lay uneasy in my bunk.

When the wind subsided I came on deck in daylight to see a surrealistic scene. The two huge swells marched across one another about half a mile apart, and where the swells met arose a series of what looked like marine Matterhorns. I have heard this described as 'clapotis' and you see it in miniature in bounce back of swells beating in a cliff and reflected back at an angle.

I did not realize their danger and started to get under way. Fortunately, I was down below, wedged against the deckhead, coiling a rope when the boat went upside down with surprising suddenness. I found myself head downwards with two solid-looking columns of green water rushing upwards through the cockpit hatches. Her bow swung violently downwards and then up she came.

The masts and vane steering were broken, but absolutely no damage was done to me or the hull.

Now back to Murphy's Third Law: 'If anything does go wrong it is usually your own fault.' I believe that if I had got under way earlier – more courage, energy and initiative – the boat, moving and presenting a dynamic rather than a static target, might well not have capsized.

Now a few words on keel design. *Galway Blazer* had a fin keel like all ocean-racing and most cruising boats. Now, I feel that a better arrangement would have been an old-fashioned long, shallow keel which, if the boat is falling down a wave, does not so much reach down into the water and trip, so adding to the capsizing moment.

Finally the rig. The Chinese sail is fully battened, the mainsail ones were 14 feet long. In those days we had not developed light man-made fibre battens sufficiently robust to stand up to the forces involved. My battens were hickory and very heavy. Although the sails were down, the heavy bundle was well above the centre of gravity as also, though less so, was the spare set carried below. All this must have added to the capsizing moment. I have dealt with this incident at greater length in a later chapter.

Heaving to My first *Galway Blazer* was an RNSA 24 foot ocean-racing cruiser, ketch rigged. While crossing the Atlantic in 1949 we ran into heavy weather – about Force 9–10 for a day.

I got down to bare poles, lashed the helm down and went below to rest. The boat sailed with the pressure of the wind on masts and hull, poked up a point or so into the wind and moved ahead at, say, half a knot. Aerodynamically, I must confess, I do not understand why she did this. I never had a moment's trepidation: the land was far enough away to cause no worry.

To sum up:

1   The measures which you take at the onset of very heavy weather must depend on the design, construction and rig of your boat, the proximity of navigational dangers, the meteorological situation as far as you can judge it and the factors of your own strength and endurance.

2   A light displacement boat is better not 'sea-anchored' by warps or drogues which may hold her down like a man in a pub fight punched against the wall; a very strong boat may do well thus.

3   For running downwind, assuming of course no dangers to leeward, you need plenty of buoyancy up forward; you must accept the disadvantage that she will 'slam' when going to windward.

4   If you decide to heave to, keep heading up to windward of the wind abeam position and keep moving. If heaving to with sails set, say, try-sail and storm jib sheeted to weather, do not sheet the storm jib so far to weather that she is blown off, beam on or beyond; this is where you get rolled over.

5   In design and stowage, strive to keep down weight situated above the centre of gravity. Strive to raise the underwater sideways centre of effort. If you want a deep keel why not a dropkeel which can be raised in these conditions?

6   Finally, ensure that nothing is stowed in the boat in such a way that it will move if the boat turns over. Many of the boats capsized or laid flat in the 1979 Fastnet Storm had their batteries break adrift, for they were not properly secured. This ideal may only

be reached in heaven, but like other ideals it can be sought. And this applies to *you* in your boat. You are at the most vulnerable when you are asleep. I had a rope round the bunk across *my* centre of gravity. When out of the bunk I was always wedged in or gripping a handhold.

CHAPTER NINE

The Wheeling Stars

In the introduction to this book I wrote in a general fashion about the emotional well-springs of lone voyaging. Now it is time to get to the root of the matter, and in this connection to describe and explain what I hinted at in an earlier chapter on loneliness; that is the comradeship which you, the sailor alone, having left your neighbours will feel with the surrounding universe which becomes in a very personal sense, your neighbourhood.

For a start, let us try to interpret what the wise Bertrand Russell, mathematician and philosopher, indicated in more than one of his works: that the only period when people were generally happy was when they all hunted for their livelihood, living in a state of nature, approximately ten thousand years ago. Such a sweeping statement requires an explanation and if I understand Russell correctly there are three reasons.

First, from philosophical deduction, people were motivated principally from passion rather than from forethought. Forethought is very likely to engender worry. Second, from observation of the very few remaining people who still depend for their existence on hunting, so long as they are not starving or interfered with by civilization they appear to be happy. Finally, historically, when the human race became successively pastoral, agricultural, commercial, industrial and highly technical, those who could afford to do so continued to hunt. Tally Ho!

An earlier philosopher and scientist, Descartes, finding himself at one point baffled by the immensity and complexity of the universe and by the impossibility of comprehending its creation and evolution or if there could be a spiritual osmosis, began to be obsessed by the idea that the whole thing was an illusion, that nothing was actually *there*. Finally, if I read him right, he was released from this mental straitjacket by this blinding glimpse of the obvious: 'I *think*, therefore I am.'

In tying up these two somewhat diverse lines of thought with the emotions of a lone sailor and with what follows, I shall in all humility coin a post-Cartesian phrase: 'I *feel*, therefore I am.' By feel, of course, I mean 'feel with my emotional sensitivity, with my passion'.

Do not imagine from all this that I advocate the total renunciation of forethought in your approach to lone sailing. Immense forethought must go into all the preparations for your voyages, which I shall detail in a later, more prosaic chapter (chap. 11). These preparations will tend greatly to diminish your happiness and, if you are anything like me, will leave you nervously shredded. Furthermore, if you run into disasters or other changed circumstances at sea, forethought will have to resurface, but in the main you may follow your intended track like a hunter on the game spoor: free from the shackles of civilization you will be at one with nature and live in a beautiful blinding swirl of colour and movement.

Before we set sail I have one reservation which is best summed up by another philosopher. Goethe wrote in *Italian Journey*, 'When I get south of the Alps I can believe in God again.' This is a sentiment which I heavily endorse and to transfer it into maritime terms the Alpine barrier will transmute into Cape Villano, which is the top left-hand corner of Spain, as you look at the map.

In all those awful seas north of Iberia I have tossed around for many periods of acute discomfort and danger: in submarines in peace and war and in a multitude of yachts of a vast range of designs and sizes. Furthermore, I have lived for the last forty years in a leaking Norman castle below the tide-line in Galway Bay. I doubt if God meant us to live in these latitudes. As a lone mariner I suggest that you regard the turbulent areas of the westerly winds as a place in which to test yourself or anything else you may wish to test, or as a place to be nervously traversed in pursuit of your goal.

Before I ask you to come south with me let us investigate another possibility. One of my friends, John Gore-Grimes, likes to sail in polar regions. He has been to Spitzbergen and Greenland and also Antarctica, which, he writes, is drier than the deserts of Arabia, sunnier than California, higher than the mountains of Switzerland,

emptier than the South Pacific and as big as the United States and
Europe put together. Dr David Lewis sailed his 32-foot sloop *Icebird*
down there alone. This was, I think, the most outstanding feat of
endurance in the annals of human adventurous effort. I am not going
to follow either of these intrepid explorers, but there remains with
me the memory of an ecstatic experience of Arctic beauty in the
unlikely environment of a submarine on war patrol.

We had been on some mission which took us within the Arctic
Circle. It was autumn and the weather was fair with a clear sky. Night
had fallen so we were on the surface, the lookouts all watchful on
their sectors. A faint light appeared in the northern sky. At first we
suspected that there was a searchlight over the horizon, but then it
slowly increased and heightened and a new scene unfolded. It was as
though some vast cosmic mother goddess stood at the apex of our
universe, trailing skirts, shot with mauve and green fire, across the
northern sky. Slowly the skirts moved in the convolutions of a celestial
saraband. The dance widened its boundary until it circled completely
around the horizon. We were a small dot in the middle of an iono-
spheric kaleidoscope. For a short while we stepped out of the war. I
hoped that any enemies who might be in the vicinity would also have
diminished their vigilance. The aurora borealis flamed coldly overhead
and as it finally faded I heard someone let out a long slow sigh.

Remember, however, that polar waters can only be reached by
traversing the windy latitudes between 40° and 60°, that the polar
regions do themselves brew up some appalling storms and blizzards,
that you may collide with partly submerged ice, that ice forms on your
deck and that it is bloody cold. Finally let us leave those thousands
of yachtsmen, some of them single-handers, thrashing about, cruising
or racing in inhospitable latitudes and make a track for happier seas.

If you start from the South Coast of England you will inevitably
have to beat round Ushant, trying to avoid the traffic separation zones
where mammoth ships, which take half an hour to stop their forward
process, mass and moan in the mists. You might expect to reach
across the Bay of Biscay, which has a villainous reputation but is
usually benign, having perhaps been enveloped by an offshoot of the
Azores high-pressure area. There will undoubtedly be a swell running
in from some distant Atlantic storm and there may be one of those

occasional errant depressions which veer south of their normal tram-line and kick up the very devil of a storm.

Cape Villano is a turning-point of winds and currents and the visibility for your landfall will probably be bad. Once past Villano you have made it. The Iberian peninsular has its own mini-climate and acts like a mini-continent. The rain in Spain actually does stay mainly in the plain, that is the northern coastal plain. Inland Spain becomes brown, dry and high. The plateau heats up in summer and hot air rises. The pressure drops and cool air tries to rush in; Coriolis Force, which I shall discuss later, twists the wind in a cyclonic direction around the low-pressure area and so you have a smart northerly wind to blow you in the direction in which you want to go. It will blow a bit fresh, but you can usually carry full sail and bat along at maximum speed. The farther out from the coast the lighter the wind will be; closer in you will get involved with shipping, which is not good for the lone sailor. You may not yet be in a maritime paradise, but the sun is warmer and the fun of going downhill is something like the joy you had the first time you rode a bicycle with hands off; the bow wave roars and you occasionally ride the crest of a wave like a surfer on a board. You are then exceeding the theoretical maximum speed of your boat and the steering blade of your vane gear emits a joyous scream like an excited child.

These winds, sometimes called the Portuguese trade winds, are meant to link up with the true north-east trade winds farther south. But although they do not, the ensuing calm gap which reaches south of Madeira is not too aggravating. Small depressions travel in and out of the Straits of Gibraltar and you can ride their winds; the current is behind you, the sun is glorious, you are not delayed for too long and exotic bird life begins to appear; dark boobies, sort of sunburned gannets, delicate white tropic birds with long pointed tails and a quarrelsome chattering nature. Once, sitting becalmed hundreds of miles from land, there descended on my deck a segmented dragonfly. Borne aloft by hot air over Africa it had wafted out to sea on a high outwelling air current and finally fluttered down in still air to visit me. I watched it turn its little head round through $180°$ to clean its back and at the same time a small blue butterfly zigzagged past. The dragonfly flew off to join it in inevitable death. I felt no sadness, they had had their happy life with no forebodings.

The next waypoint is the Canary archipelago. You may stop or you may not. If you do land, you may meet, as I did, one of the few people remaining of the indigenous Guancha race, a dark, curly-haired people with blue eyes and their own language. They are thought to be a mixture of original negroes and early colonizing Vikings. The man whom I met was proud of his exotic origins and caused me to ponder on the result of the intermingling of two such dissimilar races. But in any case you will surely sight the snow-capped peak of El Pico, Tiede, Tenerife, 12,000 feet, which you may climb to peer down into the crater of the semi-active sulphurous volcano, a grim reminder of the mouth of hell!

As the volcano slides astern below the horizon you enter the north-east trade wind belt, and this is dreamtime. Here, where our ancestors used an eternal windstream to cross to the Spanish Main, your prayers are answered for fair, steady winds. There is unfailing sun climbing ever higher; little flocky clouds scud over and break monotony, pretty blue and green fish called dorados swim around and remind you that if your food supply gives out you might catch them and live. Shearwaters perform their aerial ballet around you: when they bank to turn, the lower wing does not exactly shear but kisses the water, as though the bird rested one wing on the waves. This is a dress rehearsal for the great act which you will see if you venture into southern waters, the mighty albatross who is the prince of gliders.

The first flying fish will appear, followed by many coveys of these iridescent blue-green triers apparently becoming birds, as the flight-less penguins seem to be evolving into fish. While you watch the more successful individuals in the flying coveys, they appear to be straining to keep aloft, as indeed they are, to escape their predatory enemies, the larger fish below them. Many will later land on your deck at night to provide a delicious fish fry for breakfast.

The clouds which drive overhead do not let down their water until they reach the mountains of the Antilles, two thousand miles away, so do not enter this zone with empty water tanks; and if you are bound in that direction dip well down into the trade wind belt to 19°N. Whatever it says on the wind chart, you will tend to run out of wind north of this. If you continue southward with me, take with a pinch of salt the advice in the Admiralty publication *Ocean Passages for the World* (subsequently revised in 1987) which advises a great hook eastward towards Liberia to get well to the windward of South America. This advice was written for square-rigged ships which went badly to windward. A modern yacht can, I think, better cross the calm Doldrum belt fairly well to the westward where it is narrowest and use its own windward ability to weather the bulge of Brazil.

And now for the Doldrums, known also as the intertropical convergence zone. It is the meeting place of the north-east trade winds of the northern hemisphere with the corresponding south-east winds across the Equator. It is in the Atlantic, a little north of the Equator and moves north and south a few degrees with the sun. It continues round the world but is interfered with around Southern Asia by the monsoons. These are caused by the summer heating and winter cooling of the vast land mass centred in Mongolia, whence also you may remember, came Genghis Khan's fierce cavalry.

The Doldrums, a synonym for a state of mental depression or lethargy, is an area which was dreaded by our forefathers in sailing ships. Calm might descend for weeks, broken by irritating little local storms which got them nowhere. A heavy confused swell persisted in spite of there being no wind. This threatened to capsize a fully-rigged ship due to the weight of the spars generating rhythmic rolling. If you are in a yacht race, have a time schedule to meet or are running out of supplies, you may well inherit their irritation. I have seen, however, no record of anyone remaining there for ever and if you can stay relaxed much enjoyment can be had. Here is what I wrote in my journal when in those waters:

Sitting up on deck to watch the sunrise, I saw a vast towering mushrooming pile of ectoplasmic cloud almost right overhead for ever spewing upwards more reproductions of its lower shelf. The lower slopes were dark with white above them like some giant alp. Away to the northward another white tower reflected back the first sunrays towards me down a sinuous seapath.

Later I wrote of the sea around me:

Intrusions roll into the Doldrums like an army with endless reserves. The North Atlantic sends down the accumulated swells of its turmoil and the southern trades push up their foretelling waves. These swells run through one another and cross swells are kicked up by the passing squalls. The resulting *melange* is a series of mounds of polished basalt in the clouded dawn.

Back again to the memoirs:

The great horizontal rolls of cloud with dark columns of rain like supporting pillars increased and coalesced into one overhanging sheet undershot with what looked like rolling smoke running before a forest fire.

On another day:

Dawn came up undershooting veils of high cloud with rose and brassy tints. As the light lifted above it a little curl of cirruform cloud, left beneath the higher stratus, was etched like a silver filigree underwing. A few round grey clouds moved infinitesimally slowly under the higher sheets looking like a herd of fat oxen browsing. To the north sullen stabs of lightning lit up the mauve mass of a retreating thunderpatch which had roared over us during the night.

Sometimes the mushrooming cumulus in their great towers took on the appearance of the domes of Palladio's Venetian churches seeming to rise like bubbles in the dawn. The glow of low sunlight illuminates the Wagnerian scenes, conjures the overture to a mighty opera, gives a glimpse of Olympus or Jotenheim where gods abide.

In this circumglobal belt you are conscious of being at the heartbeat of the primary force which powers the winds and weather of our oceans; the upwelling of a vast mass of warmed air which, risen and cooled, spews aloft to north-east and south-west above and contrary to the trade winds to sink to earth in two great airfalls, eighteen hundred miles distant.

Through this variable and unpredictable belt you may pass without pause, or you may spend three weeks, as in this case. However much you can relish your surroundings, human frailty may penetrate your calm acceptance. I recall that being eager for wind I was standing on the foredeck peering at the horizon and then rejoiced to see a great line of white horses advancing towards me. I gave a hail of joy for the wind, but then my jaw dropped in disbelief at what at first seemed to be a hallucination. What had appeared to be waves were the disturbances of an enormous phalanx of porpoises advancing towards me, thousands, perhaps hundreds of thousands of mammals in loose formation: the marine equivalent of the game herds of the Serengeti. Unlike the usual playful schools they kept on with grim determined purpose, not deviating, all swimming at full speed on a steady course which I plotted: it was from the apex of the bulge of Africa to the corresponding point in South America, the shortest transatlantic crossing. They must have been migrating to new feeding grounds by the most economical route. Slowly the splashes of their plunges died away and calm reigned. What had triggered this vast tribal migration? What power gathered the cohorts together?

Eventually the Doldrums are passed and the south-east trade winds start up with amazing suddenness. They may falter awhile, but will renew and seem fresher than their northerly cousins, because you are now hard on the wind and bashing into it. In my *Galway Blazer II* the spoon-shaped bow overhang smashed into the waves. The noise, harmless but disturbing, would drive me up on deck into the spray.

Finally you weather the bulge of South America and rejoice that you are clear of the equatorial current sweeping into the Gulf of Mexico which is hurricane territory. As you move farther southward the trade wind backs, freeing you from your dead beat, and also eases.

You may now sit up on deck in the tropic night, wearing only a T-shirt and shorts; the warm air moving past, stimulates but does not distract you from contemplating the absorbing environment which can be felt as well as seen. The moonpath points, as always, straight towards you across the tumbling water.

On a northbound trip in this area I wrote in my journal:

I came on deck and gave hail to the firmament, the sickle moon has set, the whole jewelled carpet of stars is spread overhead; the Milky Way arched over our course like a giant muted rainbow; the pale Pleiades are right ahead, Orion in heroic stance over the foremast, Sirius the dog star at the main; the Southern Cross is astern and close to it a black stain on the Milky Way which is a cloud of cosmic dust.

But here we are still southbound and as you look at the Milky Way you are gazing up the axis of our galaxy: Another galaxy, the Andromeda Nebula can be glimpsed, and you can sense the immensity of the vast concourse of outward-bound galaxies more through your feeling than through your mind, which can scarcely contemplate such awe-inspiring expansion into the void. Your feeling may run back in time to the astronomical Big Bang which appears to have started it, for which perhaps the Old Testament has an allegory: 'God said let there be light and there was light.' One seems as comprehensible as the other.

The exact nature of the hereafter is a mystery, but there are two theological exactitudes which are sometimes overlooked: first, if you believe in a life after death and in the event you are not proved correct you will not be disappointed; second if you were taught the doctrine of hell as perpetual torment for eternity but cannot bring yourself to believe in such nonsense, and wake up after death and find yourself frying on a griddle it will be no use to say, 'I don't believe in this!'

Enjoy now, therefore, your earthly paradise, and perhaps your contemplation of infinity may move you as it did me. I wrote after reading one of the great philosophers: 'Now I am riveted by Pascal. When someone expounds an opinion to which one has come independently oneself, what does one say? 'He must be right!'

The factor which has induced me to give intellectual approval to religious faith is the contemplation of the whole of nature, in the immensity of the firmament, in its sub-microscopic atomic structures and infinite variety: it can't just happen by chance. There must be a designer. Pascal postulated this in about 1666 and in his argument also appears to me to have scientific insight into the existence of the undiscovered molecules. Another of his thoughts I treasure: 'It is no good trying to instil religion by terror.' You instil not religion but terror. How well if mankind had followed that reasoning.

Now I am going to leave you for I am bound, in spite of my better judgement, for the Southern Ocean, against which I previously warned you. Turn back the way you came, put into some port if you wish to revictual; stay in these magic waters for a while. I shall depart with a last entry from my journal:

I was going below for a radio time check yesterday evening but paused, riveted by the scene. Above and astern the only cloud in the sky was a wisp of very high cirruform cloud, probably a hundred miles long, like a heraldic plume of feathers; lit from below by the sunset into an array of varying pink and gold it reflected a blood-red patch into the sea already darkening into purple wine.

CHAPTER TEN

The Southern Ocean

The Southern Ocean contains an area which is infested by extremes of weather. Before we enter these desperate latitudes where storm gods rule, I intend to make an exploration into Coriolis Force (named after its discoverer), which is a secondary instigator of weather. I do this because the phenomenon was so badly explained to me in my youth that I banished it from my mind and got along for the next half century with the well-known rule of thumb, Buys Ballot's Law. This states that in the northern hemisphere if you face the wind, the centre of low pressure is roughly 100° on your right hand, and vice versa in the case of high pressure. In the southern hemisphere both directions are reversed.

Not long ago, in connection with all this, I remarked to a very distinguished airman, 'Surely you, as an aviator, must have understood Coriolis Force?' 'Well no,' he replied with a smile. 'I just got along.' So I was not the only one; but I now feel that an understanding of what is happening in the general locality is helpful to the lone sailor in an appraisal of the surrounding universe, which can turn solitary confinement into a rewarding fulfilment.

I shall set forth a simple dissertation so that people like myself who are not mathematically practised may understand it, yet hope to be sufficiently accurate to avoid annoying the experts, who in any case may wish to skip the ensuing paragraphs.

Now for the explanation: Take or imagine a rotatable school globe atlas. Place your left hand over New York with the fingers pointing northward along and parallel to its meridian of longitude, that is towards the North Pole. Place your right hand over Madrid in a similar fashion. You will notice that these cities are in roughly the same latitude. You will also notice that your hands are angled *inwards* towards one another.

Regard each hand as representing the horizontal environment of a person at its centre. If you now take your right hand away and rotate the globe through the time difference between New York and Madrid – in other words move New York in the eastward direction of the earth's rotation to the position which was previously occupied by Madrid – and keep your line of sight downward through the centre of your left hand towards the earth's centre (which is the centre of its gravitational field) you will find that your left hand will have twisted, relative to your line of sight in an anticlockwise direction.

So you may visualize your environment as a wheel, and if you could stand hovering, just above the centre of the wheel, looking outwards with a fixed line of sight, each spoke of the wheel would be moving to your *left*. Thus whoever, or whatever, is at the centre of this depicted environment is at the centre of a leftward spinning turntable. This is the first thing to grasp, and I think the most difficult is the anomaly that as you look towards the North Pole the earth is rotating towards your right, but your environment is spinning to your left. The rest is easier.

Imagine now a parcel of air in the Northern Hemisphere. The parcel may be as small as a molecule. If the molecule is in still air it will remain *in situ*, held in the earth's gravitational field. But if it finds itself in an area of high pressure which is adjacent to an area of low pressure, it will be impelled to move towards the centre of low pressure. An analogy to this is that if you blow up an air balloon to high pressure and then prick it, the air will rush out into the lower pressure of the atmosphere. So our air molecule which is in the place of low pressure will find itself moving across a fast leftward-spinning centrifuge and will, therefore, arrive at a point to the *right* of that to which it was aimed.

Take, I suggest, as an analogy, one of those fast-spinning, mound-shaped horizontal wheels which used to excite people at country fairs. Everyone got shed: but if you could sit, and this was very difficult, bang over the centre of rotation, with your centre of gravity bang over your point of support, you remained sitting and spinning. But, if for a moment, you started to move your centre of gravity outwards you would have been hurled off to the right of your intended direction.

Thus in the *Northern* Hemisphere naturally-flowing air will always be twisted towards its right. In the *Southern* Hemisphere the same process will discover that the wind is twisted towards the left of its designated track.

Thus do the winds blow round the pressure systems as previously indicated by Buys Ballot's Law; in the Northern Hemisphere anticlockwise round a low, clockwise round a high, and vice versa in the Southern Hemisphere.

There is, however, one exception to all this. If you go back to the globe and place your hands spread apart and positioned as before but at the Equator, you will find that they are not angled inwards, but that all your fingers are parallel to one another; that, therefore, if you rotate the globe as before your left hand will *not* twist. You will then correctly infer that there is *no* Coriolis Force at the Equator.

If my explanation is not sufficiently clear, or if you do not wish to bother with Coriolis Force you may perfectly well get along with Buys Ballot's Law; conversely, if you wish to study the subject with more exactitude it can be pursued mathematically. Thus armed you are in touch with your neighbourhood which is now to be the area of the Southern Ocean between 40°S and 60°S, the circuit of the 'Brave West Winds' which derive as follows:

Air which was previously described as rising in the equatorial regions, fountains out northwards and southwards. Our southward-moving portion cools aloft and cascades mostly back to earth in about 30° south and spews, some north twisted to the left to make the southeast trade winds; some south, twisted again left to make the North Westerlies. These latter meet opposing south-easterly winds blowing round the Antarctic continent where there is a high-pressure mass of cold, dense air.

These opposing winds slide along one another and form an interface along which form the travelling depressions just as you see on our northern television and newspaper weather maps; only the loops caused by the warm and cold fronts are the other way up. One always feels that our Australian cousins are hanging head downwards.

But there is also this fundamental difference. If you look at a map of the world you will see that in the Northern Hemisphere and middle latitudes the oceans, and therefore, the weather patterns, are interrupted by vast continental land masses. In the Southern Ocean, however, you may draw an unobstructed parallel of latitude in, say, 57°S, right round the world for about fourteen thousand miles. The depressions follow one another in an eternal unobstructed procession trailing their warm and cold fronts, the wind blowing first from the north-west and then from the west, and finally south-west over an endless fetch. Also, as someone pointed out to me before I set out, 'There, is no Gulf Stream down there to warm you!'

The places of greatest turbulence are where pieces of land poke down somewhat to interfere with symmetry; namely the Cape of Good Hope; Cape Leeuwin (SW Australia), the Southern Cape of Tasmania; Stewart Island, the southern point of New Zealand, and (with bated breath) Cape Horn.

At the Horn there are further complications. The Antarctic continent pokes up a peninsula to within about 400 miles of the tip of South America, thus throttling the depressions into a wind funnel; the wind-driven eastgoing current meets the continental shelf, wells up and increases speed to 3 knots. The south-west wind shrieks from the polar icecap, the north-westers blow down from the Andes glaciers. Vito Dumas, who pioneered a lone voyage round this circuit in 1942, described it as 'The Impossible Route'.

Before setting out to sail a 4½-ton boat in the wake of the great square-rigged grain ships, you need some explanation or excuse above and beyond the lure of the wheeling stars.

It is possible to search backwards once again into our roots – the happy, hunting, primitive man. Two powerful urges were inherited from our animal ancestors, or if you prefer to disbelieve in evolution, were injected into Adam at the fall: sex for the continuation of the race and male aggression as a survival factor. To digress briefly about the former, I cannot help wondering how women put up with it; childbirth, I mean. What do they get? Nine months of discomfort, hours of pain, days of depression, two years or more of dirty nappies and fifty years worrying about delinquency and danger. None the less here we are, the instincts are strong. Male aggression was needed in primitive men to hunt the bison, to fight predatory animals and to wrest the cave from the bear.

With the onset of civilization and population increase came war; tribal wars for possession of land. As communities coalesced, wars became more and more severe and widespread, culminating in the holocausts of revolutions and wars of our century resulting in the deaths of approximately one hundred million men, women and children. Suddenly it is all over.

With the advent of the threat of nuclear devastation, war between the major powers is not possible, provided that the ultimate in crass political stupidity is avoided. As it happens, no major war has occurred for more than forty years. But what about aggression? It is not possible to gainsay the fact that since 1945 the so-called civilized countries have been engulfed by a rising tide of civil violence.

Many men can sublimate their aggression in a wide range of activities, spiritual, intellectual, artistic, political, industrial and social; many more simply cannot. Competitive games, which once gave a name to the chivalrous behaviour known as sportsmanship, have now become hotbeds of acrimony and financial degradation. Aggressive violence erupts in a wide range of effects; criminality, political extremism, monstrous sexual deviation, driving motor vehicles dangerously and, perhaps most disturbing but more easily linked to inbuilt aggression, mindless, apparently purposeless violence such as football hooliganism. Is it perhaps no coincidence that crazed football hooliganism is at its worst in Britain, while the European countries circled around the Alps have an easy access, for young people, to participate in the activity of downhill skiing?

Think carefully about this before you decide that I am talking through my hat, and think also of our island alternative, the sea around us. You may well say that in producing this argument I shall have to backtrack on my previous objection to our cold stormy latitudes; and so I shall, ascribing this to my excessively low blood pressure. Assuming that there is force in my point of view and relating the Southern Ocean to the problem of civil violence, I am not offering a blueprint for setting the world to rights because I am not qualified so to do. Perhaps I am nervous of being shot at from both ends of the political spectrum – those who believe that public money should not be spent and those who believe that people should not help themselves but surrender their welfare to the state. I shall, however, make a few suggestions.

To tackle the Southern Ocean alone in a glorified kayak is, of course, absolute adventure; it is a *pointer*. It seems to me that adventure is the key to the problem of unresolved male aggression, the unloading of a safety valve which has become throttled.

An enormous increase in opportunity for sail training is within the bounds of possibility; at the moment only the surface is being scratched. All round the coasts of the affluent countries lie trillions of pounds worth of yachts, many of which seldom put to sea – marine jewellery in fact. With the co-operation of owners, public bodies and with vast insurance schemes I believe that they might put usefully to sea and supplement publicly-funded sail-training vessels. Finally, the low-budget lone sailors are the windsurfers; they require sailboards, wet suits, training and, of course, large segregated areas and a corresponding increase in rescue services.

Now let us leave all this and move below 40° south, where waves roll round the world. I am surprised and ashamed to admit that I spent many years peering rather nervously at waves without fully understanding their nature. I found that there was a crumb of comfort for the ignorant from the professionals in a confession that 'The way in which the wind produces waves on the sea surface is still not completely understood.' What is certain is that if you imagine yourself in a situation of facing at right angles to a simple wave train which is moving towards your right, and then imagine your eye at the centre of a wave, every molecule of water would at that instant be describing a clockwise circle around your eye. Thus, in the bottom of the wave and in the ensuing trough, the molecules are moving towards your left. There is, albeit a slight, pathshift downwind which represents surface drift. But if you transfer back to a small boat sitting in a trough, the next wave, which appears to be the size of a cathedral, is not rushing towards you in its entirety.

For a rough analogy, take a length of rope laid straight on a flat surface. Seize one end and agitate your hand up and down rhythmically. Waves run along the rope until it looks like a cartoon serpent, but the rope does not move forward. The greatest danger of wave motion in the open ocean lies in the confusion caused by different wave trains running along or across one another, causing freak formations of very high, very steep and unruly breakers.

In addition to this, even in a regular wave train, the wave crests will break sometimes with appalling violence. This occurs when the height of the waves proportional to their length has risen to a steepness gradient of 1 to 13. But when you surf down the front of one of these giants in a swirl of white water, with your speedometer needle hard against the stop, the slope appears to your frightened glance to be far steeper than that. In the same way a very steep snow slope on a mountain appears to be at a steeper angle than that at which snow will actually lie.

My own first visit to the Roaring Forties met with total rejection. I had barely poked my nose below 39°S when the ocean really got up and hit me. In the early 1930s I had spent two or three years in a submarine flotilla on the China coast in the regular path of the typhoons without ever experiencing one of these meteorological monsters; now, being out of the area of tropical revolving storms, I met my first full-blooded hurricane.

On Thursday 30 October 1969 the barometer started to plummet downwards. As the wind's howl rose, I reefed down through gale to storm force. Finally I had just the peak of the foresail showing at about Force 10; but still it increased, with huge slabs of foam down the backs of the waves, the tops flying away and long rolls of breaking crests. I doused the foresail and ran on under bare poles. Finally a new note of scream came into the wind and the sea started to come right away in spindrift. The boat had behaved beautifully, running downwind with the vane steering working.

But this new hurricane speed defeated the vane, which could not steer, nor could the control work. I had to steer. I stood up with my head in the perspex dome, feeling remote and detached from the storm. I think it was the most thrilling experience I have ever had. I estimated the wave height at 40 feet but when the hurricane arrived all pattern seemed lost in a confusion of tumbling hills. The wind scream changed to a dull booming roar. In the very middle of the hurricane the sky had cleared and I saw a full moon glowing coldly, detached from the awful scene. In one patch of moonlight as we came down off the top of a monster I distinctly saw a petrel flying across my path below me. I recalled that a flying fish did once fly above me.

At about 5 a.m. the wind eased and the vane took over again, though its worm control was still stiff. I found that I could work it by waiting until the boat was under the lee of a particularly steep sea.

0930   There was an increase again to full violence, greater than before, the wind backing south-westerly and the barometer rising steeply. Everything which the tempest had done until then was eclipsed by the fury of two enormous seas running across one another. Every now and then the waves formed a pointed mountain of breaking water. I had wished to run downwind, steering to keep the wind on one quarter. However, I only found it possible to steer roughly downwind, worming either side of the downwind course in a spiral track; yes, literally spiral considering the huge movement out of the horizontal plane.

By now I found myself becoming very exhausted and saw that the foresail had broken loose and was liable to flog itself to death. I decided to heave to and then discovered that a two-masted junk, with the windage of the masts well forward, will only lie ahull, beam on to the seas, will not poke up to windward nor move forward as I wished to do. This was my big mistake, Murphy's Third Law again. I should have had sufficient vitality left to steer until the wind eased enough for the vane to take over, and I had a spare foresail.

Towards the evening of 31 October, Hallowe'en, 'the dead of the ghosts' high noon', the wind started to die down. I took the hurricane hatches off and went aft to tinker with the vane steering control. Then as if led by a guardian angel I returned to the enclosed cockpit for a length of rope with which to secure the foresail. I was standing jammed into place by the open hatches, coiling down the rope, when the cockpit became a cocktail shaker. Over she went to 90°. The boat was now lying on her side. Hurled by the elemental forces of the breaking peak of a rogue sea mountain she was using her side as a surfer would his board to accelerate down the face of a wave. The masts were in the air, their proper element, and I had time to think 'She will come back, that great lead keel will swing her upright.'

Even as the thought crossed my mind a vast new force started to act upon us. In those confused seas there was no proper pattern. A huge cross-riding lump of foam-lashed water rode across the trough in which we might have recovered. Into this obstacle the masts now buried themselves, driven by the frightful impetus of a sideways rush. The leverage of a new element, imposed on our mastheads, started the action of the mariner's most dreaded catastrophe – a complete roll over upside down.

I had a rapid change of mind, 'She will come back again' became 'No she won't' and indeed she did not . . .

I will not recount the subsequent recovery and limping progress with broken masts back to safety in Cape Town as it is long and boring and full of self-pity. Also I did not include this incident in my chapter on 'Disasters' (Chap. 7) as it was really not so.

I had an inbuilt rescue apparatus for the emergency. This was a prefabricated jury mast consisting of a bipod constructed of two 'Proctor' tubular spars, joined at one end, located in the bows. The spars were splayed with their bases pointing aft and resting on the deck. Each base was founded on a track with horizontal athwartships holes to take bolts, and thus the frame could be positioned as desired and when hoisted and stayed was a prefabricated jury mast. I have never-failing admiration for seamen who fashion jury masts from bits and pieces. In my case it was all there, and I recommend some such arrangement for anyone contemplating a long offshore voyage especially if shorthanded or alone.

By strange chance this ultimate storm was never repeated in my subsequent entire circuit of the Southern Ocean. I went carefully through the statistics in the pilot charts of the frequency of winds of gale force and above. By calculating the time likely to be spent on the various legs of the course I arrived at a probability of encountering a total of thirty-six gales or storms. Each time it blew Force 8 or above I made a pencilled ring on the chart in that area. When I left the Roaring Forties I counted the rings. There were thirty-six. It never again blew a hurricane, and I found that my little boat was beautifully adapted to running down the considerable seas which were generated.

The general pattern governed by the unobstructed weather path is that of stylized depressions. They seemed regular and the fronts march along like columns of cavalry in line abreast. There was mostly sufficient separation between the fronts so that the wave trains were not interfering too much with one another. The boat acted like the perfect surf board. The faster she surfed off the tops of very long lines of breaking crests, the better she steered. On one occasion I heard on the radio of a severe depression which had stopped a cricket match in Melbourne, brought snow in midsummer to Tasmania, causing flooding in Brisbane and hammered the fleet in the Sydney–Hobart Race.

I was awaiting it, being south of New Zealand, and sure enough I could see the storm clouds piling up to the west. The wind arrived with great suddenness and I could hear it approach with a sinister snarling noise, the seas still short and confused but very determined. The splendid Hasler vane self-steering gear would nearly always co-operate, but at above 50 knots over the deck the friction drive slipped as a safety measure, so that in some storms manual steering became essential.

Occasionally, too, if she did not pick up enough speed on a wave crest she would tend to broach and manual override on the helm was needed. This happened seldom, mostly in the final traumatic dash around Cape Horn. Here queues of depressions had closed up.

The fronts followed one another with eager tenacity of purpose. The wind slammed across as each one passed and visibility closed in to about 400 yards. I had the standard hallucination of thinking someone else was aboard, particularly when down below doing careful calculations of estimated positions; I thought the other chap was keeping a lookout in case we hit South America.

I had very good confidence in the latitude sight which had passed me safely between Diego Ramirez and Ildefonso; but longitude which depended on correct assessment of the distance run became very important. If I turned left too soon I should hit a continent instead of breaking out into the broad Atlantic. I gave Cape Horn a board of 20 miles for safety and carefully worked out the estimated positions as we drove frantically downwind, mostly under bare poles. Occasionally it eased between fronts and I would set some sail. The Horn current can run at 3 knots, but one must *know when* you are in its influence. There is an air station at Ushuaia, not far north, but its beacon only transmits when the weather is fit for flying.

It was not. There is, however, another beacon at Punta Arenas, but this is hundreds of miles away over the mountains and I did not expect it to be audible. I tried it, however, and by some miracle received it loud and clear. The bearing passed exactly through my estimated position. I based my time to turn to the northward on this position and after a somewhat anxious period of peering into the mist, the great swells of the Southern Ocean subsided. I realized that I now had the South American continent as a breakwater against the eternal eastward-driven waves.

But the tempest does not blow for ever. A total of thirty-six gales and storms over a run of fourteen thousand miles gives room for plenty of spells of reasonable weather when there is time to admire the wealth of bird life that populates the vast arena surrounding the Antarctic continent, like a gigantic aviary.

No one could watch the wandering albatross flying close alongside and remain unmoved. This huge, beautiful tapered bird, with a 12-foot wingspan, hangs serene in motionless flight gliding on the air-wave ahead of each giant swell. The birds follow in friendly proximity, seem to attach themselves for a day or so and then depart to be succeeded by more, whose varying stages of maturity can be gauged by their colouring and size. The young are marked by black patches which slowly disappear; the mature male is perfectly white – with a black wing border, the female has a black dot on her head.

They glide along one wave, turn over it banking to brush the water with a wingtip and glide back along the next wave; or ride the boat's slip-stream, turning a head to take in all that is going on, often alighting on the water in breaking crests up to 40 knots of wind.

I nearly ran down a pair doing what looked like a courting routine, bill crossing, but they were thousands of miles from land and their breeding grounds.

Small, dark, fluttering, the tiny petrel is a total contrast to the gliding giants. I never ceased to look on them with wonderment. How can this bird, the smallest variety hardly larger than a starling, sustain the energy of perpetual motion? Mariners have always loved them, called them petrels after St Peter from their habit of appearing to try to walk on the water, actually stirring the microlife to feed. They were also called Mother Carey's chickens, an anglicization of *Mater Cara*, beloved mother, the Mother of God. I read in some bird book that they never alight on the water, but I have seen them sitting, although only in flat calm. Their cousins, the prions, are more gregarious and flock in great bodies. The dove prions delight the eye in mass manœuvres; their blue tops melt into the background sky as they bank round you, then the whole flock turns instantaneously, presenting white undersides, and there appears a flurry of snowflakes. Another type, the whale bird, scoops up sea-water with its nose and has an internal apparatus similar to a whale to filter out the plankton.

The great variety of subspecies of albatross, petrels and prions presents a never-ending identification parade; indeed for me they merged, as the sooty albatross, small and dark, was indistinguishable from the giant petrel.

Referring back to my earlier claim to immunity from loneliness, I wonder in retrospect if sailing these vast deserted waters might have chilled the mind were it not for the never-failing company of all those living creatures whose flight has over the centuries stimulated artistry, religion and man's urge to move in a new element.

CHAPTER ELEVEN

Minding Yourself

Preceding chapters have dealt with how to conduct and survive a long singlehanded voyage through all kinds of weather and adversities. Now I shall focus on the sort of regime and precautions I found necessary for my safety and well-being. Some of my solutions may not suit everyone and may even be contentious.

To start with the vexed question of alcohol. In this context I recall an anecdote about a distant relative. She was a splendid lady, devoutly religious in the old-fashioned Church of England vein. She was also a strict teetotaller to the point of being an abolitionist. At some grand party her dinner companion asked her, 'But Lady B, how do you reconcile your view on alcohol with the Miracle at Cana when Our Lord turned the water into wine?' There was a hush in the general conversation, but no lack of sound or authority in the reply which rang in the ears of an astonished audience: 'A very notable lapse of judgement on the part of Our Lord.'

While not entirely subscribing to this viewpoint, I was to a certain extent influenced by my mentor John Illingworth. John enjoyed greg-arious conviviality in harbour or ashore, but when *Myth of Malham* prepared for a race everything was sacrificed to the purity of the purpose, which was to win the race. No booze was allowed on board. I heard much later in life that this rule did deter one or two prospective crew members.

Some also complained that John would allow you to take a tooth-brush, but would drill holes in the handle to reduce weight. Be all that as it may, I took no booze to sea in *Galway Blazer II*. People said to me, 'But would you not take some medicinally?' Actually I think it is bad medicine, though excellent for oiling the wheels of social converse, or embellishing a good meal. It is also a good anaesthetic.

Dr David Lewis, who is as you may have guessed one of my heroes, took some strong rum with him in *Icebird* to the Antarctic and used it to good effect when he was in such extremes of cold and exhaustion as would have long since converted me into frozen meat. Dr Lewis is, I guess, one of those rare people, like Bill Tilman, who surface every now and then, a being impervious to cold, heat, exhaustion and other slings and arrows of outrageous fortune. Everything nourishes the strong. Remembering all this, one must adjust the use of alcohol to one's own ethics and mental and physical tolerance.

Food, which I consider should be a pleasurable but efficient personal fuel, also attracts a great deal of emotion. The obvious points to consider are: What food do you like? What do you think is good for your health? What food is allowed by your ethical or religious principles? How and where can you stow enough for a long voyage? How can you get food if you are beset or your supply runs out? And what about preparation and cooking? All this has to be thought out at a personal level, but one important fact must never be forgotten: the threat of scurvy.

It is well known that in the days of long voyages in sailing ships when fresh food, the source of vitamin C, could not be carried in sufficient quantity owing to restricted storage space and deterioration young, strong, healthy men working in the fresh air on physical tasks died like flies of vitamin C deficiency.

It is now generally agreed that the members of Scott's last expedition to the South Pole also died of this disease, existing as they did largely on tinned food. Amundsen, who came out alive, took with his team a quantity of dried fruit. During the last war (summer 1940) in a submarine flotilla operating off the coast of Norway, in circumstances where every possible moment had to be spent submerged with little oxygen to breathe, a very high casualty rate and only tinned food to eat, incipient scurvy was diagnosed among the crew: gums bled, teeth loosened, cuts and wounds were slow to heal. The issue of dehydrated vegetables put an end to it. Dried food apparently retained vitamins better than tinned food in that era.

Remembering that another of my paragons, Sir Francis Chichester, had grown cress as an antiscorbutic, I followed suit with bags of compost and little plastic gardens. However, when I was rolled over in a hurricane the compost spread itself in a paste over the deckhead and seeped into lockers, forming unwanted mud patches.

In subsequent voyages I substituted mung beans, the kind you get in a Chinese take-away. The trick is to get a half-pound Kilner jar, drill holes in the cap for air, secure it by shock cord on a platform exposed to light, put in some beans and damp them. Experience will teach you how much water to add: too little and they won't sprout, too much and they drown and go sour. Just right they grow well in temperate climes, like triffids in the tropics, but near the Antarctic they won't grow at all. So although I am averse to pills, I then took vitamin tablets.

It is with some reluctance that I recount what food I actually took, apart from mung beans, because it would, I think, suit no one else. It did, however, solve the problems of stowage, preparation, cooking and washing up – all reduced to the utmost simplicity or obviated. The diet was Australian sultanas and raisins, very large and good quality, and cartons of a paste consisting of whole almond nuts ground very fine. The dried fruit was reconstituted by soaking overnight in a Kilner jar, the nut paste spooned out and mixed with water to the consistency of cream. All was then mixed up in a mug into a sort of Christmas-pudding-like mush and eaten; one mug for breakfast, one for midday and one for the evening meal.

Bizarre as this sounds, I found it satisfying and kept in perfect health throughout my voyages. The only other addition was fried fresh flying fish and a few wholemeal biscuits. I discovered that this diet would not be universally popular when my son came out to Cape Town to help me repair the boat after capsizing, to get her back to England to remast and start afresh.

We worked on into the dinner hour and I said, 'Well, let's just have a picnic of the boat's food.' After a few spoonfuls my son announced politely, 'I think I'll just slip off for lunch at the yacht club.' Again in Perth, Western Australia, the boat was the guest of the hospitable Royal Freshwater Bay Yacht Club. My wife was with me and we invited a friend to lunch at the club. When she arrived we found that the club did not do lunches on Wednesdays. I said lightly, 'We'll eat the boat's food.' I noticed that our guest's spoon was slowing down. Finally she said, 'I think I'll just have a cup of coffee.' So this is why I leave you to work out your own menus, but do remember vital vitamin C.

It is important to visualize how you may keep alive if your embarked food supply has failed; and this applies both to your boat and, in case of total shipwreck, to whatever life-raft you may carry. The history of marine survival recounts many instances of people who have survived for incredible periods and over very long distances in purpose-built life-rafts, inflatable craft or flotation units cobbled up from wreckage. A good supply of fishing lines and spoon bait is needed and one or more knives with, preferably, flotation handles. A ready-made plankton-catching net can be fashioned from a muslin bag mounted on a wire ring with suitable towing attachments.

Trolling for fish is normally only effective at slow speeds and, of course, the plankton net will only work at very slow speed. Obviously a survival kit should be stowed in or near the survival craft, or in a handy position, and should include some fresh-water supply.

I embarked a wetsuit and, for shark fighting, an 18-inch Bowie knife, well balanced and somewhat like a Gurkha's kukri. Both these were unfortunately stolen in Australia.

You can live a very long time without food, but not for long without fresh water, or food with high water content.

Against medical opinion, I tend to exist normally on a low average fluid intake. I found that at sea my daily ration was one small mug of hot drink at each meal plus what was required to reconstitute the dried fruit, cream the nut paste and water the beans: somewhere between one and two pints daily. On another occasion I recall, in mid-Atlantic in a crewed yacht, we ran out of fresh water due to a plumbing fault, and I then had a gloomy recollection of Coleridge's Ancient Mariner, 'Water, water, everywhere, Nor any drop to drink.'

The measures which you should take are as follows: have a design of boat with adequate fixed fresh-water tanks, totally clean and filled with sweet, not distilled, water, which latter does leach minerals from the body. It is important for the supply to be subdivided in case a tank goes wrong; and not to have an electric pump which is activated by a pressure drop so that a broken pipe may cause your water to disappear into the bilges. Carry reserves of fresh water in plastic cans, well stored and lashed down; investigate methods of catching rain water from deck or sails and see what is the latest in gadgets for distilling fresh water from sea-water, which improve as time goes on.

Remember, above all, that if you are badly beset, the tendency is to die of fear before collapsing from hunger or thirst. The adage about not drinking sea-water must apply, though I consider insufficient research has gone into the reason why Dr Bombard was able to adjust to this forbidden practice while drifting across the Atlantic on an inflatable.

Assuming that all is well with the commissariat, the most important consideration is to avoid personal injury. I cannot emphasize too strongly the importance of sufficient handholds in the boat, both above and below decks. These are frequently inadequate in standard designs and in my own boat, having strongly stressed this point in design and building, I found myself fashioning two more for the high-risk moment of entering the cabin hatchway while at sea.

At sea in rough weather you must so conduct yourself that the boat may perform any sudden gyration without throwing you violently against some hard projection. On deck there is, in addition to the risk of injury, that of falling over the side, where the boat will sail away from you. This leads to another vexed question – guard rails and clip-on lifelines.

I imagine that *Galway Blazer II* was probably unique in having no guard rails and, therefore, an explanation is required. The advantages claimed are: saving in expense and top weight, elimination of the risk of damage to the deck which occurs if a guard rail stanchion is strained, the elimination of a mental attitude that the guard rail is a total safety net, which it is not, and elimination also of the temptation to clip a safety belt on to the guard rail, which is highly dangerous. In a boat of heavy scantlings, of course, the deck fittings of the stanchions can be strong, but *Galway Blazer II* was of ultra-light construction.

This brings us to the subject of clipping on, which I believe I invented in 1949, but which claim I have heard to be hotly contested. Shortly after the Second World War I acquired an RNSA 24-foot cruiser/ocean racer, *Galway Blazer*, to sail across the Atlantic. I fitted her out to be sailed alone, but in the event I took with me a remarkably courageous man, Guy Cole. Guy had been crippled by polio from infancy, but was determined for adventure. In those days, ocean racing and cruising crews did not, in my experience, use safety lines, but relied on agility and balance to remain on board.

Realizing that, if Guy did fall overboard he would have no chance of survival, and not wishing to burden him with a permanently-worn life jacket I rigged two wire jackstays along the deck, one either side of the mast, for the length of the boat. These were drawn up bar taut with cod-line lizards. By clipping on to either of these one could range the deck like a tethered goat. The modern prefabricated line with clip hook has one or more set lengths. My primitive outfit was simply a bowline round the waist. Thus the length was adjustable to the requirement of the moment. The line could be used in tension to lean against, with of course the disadvantage that time had to be spent adjusting it.

This brings us to the question of whether the safety line is actually desirable. There is a school of thought which argues that, tethered as you are with the line apt to foul objects in the dark, you are that much more seamanlike without one. Well, we had a naval saying, 'different ships, different longsplices'. In *Galway Blazer II* I retained the tethered-goat outfit and also my adjustable lifeline in preference to the modern fixed fitting, the argument being that if the line is always taut you do not run the risk of being flung by a wave and then brought up with fearful retardation at the end of the scope of your line.

Another feature of *Galway Blazer II* which raised a few eyebrows was the whale-backed deck. The slope towards the sea on either side appeared to shed one. However, when heeled, of course, the weather slope became more or less horizontal, an advantage over conventional boats whose decks are then canted. Running downwind in heavy weather there is, of course, no such advantage and I was frequently reduced to a hands and knees progression along the deck.

Having decided your options on these issues the next problem is what equipment you should take with you for repairs, renewals or to combat disaster. Faced with a wealth of advice from many expert sources one might feel inclined to tow another boat astern containing a complete ship's chandler's stock-in-trade. I am hesitant about making a list, which is always liable to be incomplete or contain redundancies, but there are some principal requirements which have general application:

Spare rope and wire of the necessary sizes with splicing equipment.

Destruction tools to cut loose mast and rigging in case of dismasting.

Space blanket.

A sail repair outfit.

Tools for shipwright's repair use.

If you carry machinery or high technology gear, the necessary spares and repair gear.

Appropriate fire extinguisher.

Fire blanket.

Timber.

Wedges.

Wooden plugs of various appropriate sizes.

One or two triangular collision mats with eyelets at each corner. After my disaster I carried these; to replace the oakum thrums of the old naval article, I had on one an offcut of deep pile carpet sewn on, and on the other some foam rubber covered with canvas (but foam rubber does tend to disintegrate with age).

The necessary spares for your electrical equipment and electrical maintenance, soldering equipment and multimeter.

Storage battery maintenance gear, unless you have modern sealed batteries; batteries must be battened so that they do not move in case of capsize.

Spares and tools for repair and maintenance of machinery and drill (hand or power).

Torches.

Spare batteries and a head torch.

A supply of nails, screws, nuts, bolts and tacks, shims and washers.

A come-in-handy locker, bag or box.

A supply of shock cord of appropriate sizes.

Lubricants and adhesives.

Where applicable a fibreglass repair outfit (but how do you repair fibreglass at sea when water splashes over?) A copper tingle might be fixed using a power drill and self-tapping screws – very difficult alone. Could one, I wonder, use underwater cement clamped on by the collision mat principle?

I cannot emphasize too strongly the principle of not overcrowding your boat, of having everything well stowed and, thus, having plenty of clear working space in which to perform in emergency. Also, remember most of the gear which you carry is top weight, which can add to the capsizing moment.

The Rip Van Winkle Syndrome can be diagnosed in the case of an old sailor who went to sea in the stick and string era and then went to sleep for a hundred years. On waking up he found difficulty in adjusting to, say, an ocean racer of the later 1980s, whose equipment has the technology of a spacecraft. I may lay myself open to accusations of being in this sort of situation by a general thread of aversion to technicality running through the previous chapters; further weight may be added to this view by the information that, of the three boats which I have owned, *Tre Sang* 30 square metres, *Galway Blazer* an RNSA 24-footer and *Galway Blazer II* a 4½-ton junk, none was designed with either a propulsive engine or fitted heads.

The disadvantages of engines are expense, top weight, fire risk, holes in the hull, noise, and smelly atmospheric pollution. An engine may well get one out of a jam and can be a great convenience, particularly if you need to charge batteries. Conversely if you have to rely on sail, as did our ancestors, you do sharpen up your seamanship.

The heads carry the same disadvantages of expense and top weight and the added greater risk of leakage in through the hull fittings. I read that Francis Chichester nearly had his boat sunk at sea through the heads. I myself was aboard *Mischief*, an old boat which I believe once belonged to Tilman. After completion of a short cruise most of the crew departed and I was asleep on board alongside the jetty in Southampton. I was awoken by gurgling and splashing. Looking over the side of my bunk I saw water, the level of which was rising visibly. I jumped out, rushed to the heads to shut the hull valve of the water inlet. It seemed immobile and not to have been worked since it had been fitted. I looked around for a wheel spanner, ubiquitous in a submarine. But we were not in a submarine. I adapted a large adjustable spanner to fit the wheel of the valve and swung on it praying that the shaft would not snap. There was, of course, no danger to life but one would have looked very silly having the boat sink alongside the jetty. The shaft held and the valve shut off. This incident converted me to the bucket-and-chuck-it school of thought.

If you have no engine in a light boat it is essential to carry a propulsive unit to move short distances when becalmed. *Tre Sang* with very low freeboard carried a pair of oars and I was able to row her for about 2 miles across the dead water, the tidal meeting place in the Irish Sea, at high tide and thus caught the southward ebb instead of being carried northward whence I had come. *Galway Blazer*, with medium freeboard, carried a Red Indian canoe paddle and with this I was able to shift berth in Gibraltar harbour in a calm. *Galway Blazer II* had very high freeboard and I foolishly neglected to fit a stern sweep or Chinese sampans 'yulow' for these will propel a light, easily-driven hull quite efficiently. I found myself embarrassingly becalmed in the Solent in the path of a giant liner, and on another occasion, when becalmed in the Needles Channel by Hurst Castle in a strong flood tide, the boat was swept against a channel buoy and suffered some damage; one would only have had to move her for one boat's length to avoid collision.

The bucket-and-chuck-it organization requires a permanent housing for the bucket. In my case it was under a flap-up step in the access to the hatch; and a large supply of newspaper with which to line the bucket for sanitary purposes; of course, if other folk are aboard privacy is apt to be lost. In this connection I recall an adventurous clergyman who walked across the Sahara pushing his supplies in a Chinese wheelbarrow with a squaresail for downwind work. He fell in with Bedouin and observed that in the Sahara there were no bushes or rocks behind which you may retreat; to obtain privacy one would have to walk over the horizon, so men, women and children just do their business where they are without embarrassment.

To revert to the Rip Van Winkle disease and to rebuff the suspicion that I may be an advanced case, let me assure you that I recognize man's inventive genius has made tremendous strides over the centuries. One might specify in particular the wheel and the disposable nappy. In the last forty years sophisticated equipment has improved and multiplied in response to the population explosion of yachts. I am in favour of seeking out the most up-to-date but well-tried gear which may contribute to safety, comfort and efficiency. Obviously you must decide whether you really need it, can afford it, can conveniently fit it, and details of spares and servicing. Consider the battery power it may need and, above all, realize that it may break down irretrievably and you are then back to first principles, which should never be lost sight of or allowed to become unpractised.

That is not to say that I share the views of Mr Thomas Hood, navigator of a squadron of privateers bound for China in 1582. He scorned books on navigation saying, 'I will not give a fart for all their cosmography, for I can tell more [by intuitive judgement?] than all the cosmographers in the world.' He got hopelessly lost off West Africa and ended up where he had started, in Plymouth.

The most pressing requirement is a means of recharging batteries. Very efficient models driven by wind or water are now available. Solar panels are another system. Armed with any of these at least, a bright masthead strobe light could be permanently lit at night. I should like to see fitted the new device (ARGOS) which enables a shore station to keep track of the boat's exact position at any moment. This alone made it possible for Richard Broadhead in *Perseverance* to rescue the French naval officer, Jacques de Roux, in the Southern Ocean, whose yacht had been dismasted and was in a sinking condition 300 miles away. My imagination boggles at the thought of finding a yacht without a mast in those huge seas, and I can't help thinking that some extra-sensory link was also involved. Jacques de Roux went to the well once too often: he lost his life during the 1986 single-handed race round the world when only 200 miles from Sydney.

One can keep up to date with new developments by browsing round the London Boat Show; in 1988 I was much taken with an improved vane steering system – Hydrovane YXA self-steering which can compete with hurricane-force winds and has successfully stood the ultimate test of a non-stop round-the-world passage, south of the Five Capes, by Leslie Powles.

THEFT AND PIRACY

I was lax in my attitude to theft from my boat while in port. *Galway Blazer II* was berthed alongside a pontoon astern of a submarine depot ship in Devonport. I felt she was fairly secure. Apart from thieves on gainful forays one has to envisage souvenir hunters. Being half Irish and half Scottish by birth I planned to sail under two flags, an Irish tricolour to starboard and a red ensign to port. This might have been highly dangerous in certain waters involving fire from both banks of the river. It is also illegal. One has to fly the ensign of the country in which the vessel is registered. Well, in order to save money, I did not register *Galway Blazer II* and after dismasting passed immigration and customs in Cape Town with a passport and a Bible! When it was time to cast off and sail from Devonport, some souvenir hunter had snaffled my red ensign. *Galway Blazer II* was the first yacht to sail the route Plymouth-to-Plymouth south of the Five Capes. The first boat under 5 tons so to do and now the first under the Irish tricolour flown with doubtful legality. When we got to sea I went to the locker where I had stowed a big lump of tallow to lubricate the mainsail mast parrels and there it was not.

The theft of my wetsuit and shark-fighting knife in Fremantle, West Australia, when I temporarily left the boat unlocked was in fact not a disaster, as they never became necessary. The lesson learned is that as a single-hander in harbour you must have a reliable lock-up organization and use it when you leave the boat unguarded for anything over fifteen seconds, otherwise you may find yourself in mid-ocean lacking some vital equipment. If the locks are broken by a determined thief you will at least be alerted.

PIRACY

A helpless lone victim will be more attractive to sea raiders who are sensitive to the risks of crews summoning help by radio or even offering armed resistance. The single-hander should avoid areas where in the adjoining countries there is civil unrest or instability, oppressive regimes, entrenched drug barons or where piracy is endemic. In these places officials, fishermen and pirates are apt to be synonymous. The threat is probably most pressing in parts of the Caribbean, the Red Sea and East of Singapore.

I read of a single-hander threatened by attack off Sri Lanka. He caused the raiders to withdraw by bobbing down the after hatch and appearing up the fore hatch, differently dressed, to give an impression of numbers. Then he shouted on deck into a mock radio transmitter apparently calling for help and giving the number of the fisherman's sail. Another skipper, delivering a yacht from Japan with a crew, told me that he gave the China coast a board of some hundreds of miles and carried a licensed elephant rifle. Pirates are, however, liable to have machine-guns and one has sometimes to balance the dangers of the sea against the violence of the enemy. Is it preferable to round the Cape of Good Hope or sail down the Red Sea?

SUNK!

So your boat is sunk in mid-ocean; something has to be done besides trying to ring up God or the insurance company. With hindsight I realize that I was very lax in this department, rescue I mean. I carried a very small one-man inflatable, designed to rescue fighter pilots who parachuted into the sea when their aircraft became uncontrollable. They would mostly be a short range from their base or aircraft-carrier and could hope for quick assistance. In choosing this inadequate craft I was influenced perhaps by an obsession against carrying too much top weight and clutter and also by soaring costs of the whole project. I had a vague idea that the life raft might provide a buffer if one was cast up on a rocky shore. If I had had an EPIRB to broadcast and pinpoint my position it might have had some use in the ocean.

There have been considerable improvements in inflatables recently and a friend of mine, Enda O'Coineen, made a North Atlantic crossing in one. So I think one should carry a viable rescue craft with perhaps a sail and cover from the elements, and a survival kit. In nearly all classic survivals, drifting castaways have reached land or focal points for shipping by drifting along ocean currents, so I think that the survival kit should contain a general chart of prevailing ocean currents. In this context one must emphasize the importance of the plastic bag in which equipment can be sealed against moisture and this indeed may also apply to much within the boat herself. I learned this lesson the hard way, on land, mountaineering in New Zealand. I was swept off my feet in a flash flood and my clothes and sleeping bag were soaked. Of course, it never happened *after* I sealed everything up waterproof.

The size and type of rescue craft must depend on what you can afford and the stowage space available. If it is stowed below you must not risk an accidental automatic inflation which will jam it in place, and perhaps you behind it. On deck it is top weight and ferocious seas may work it loose and sweep it away. Multi-hulls, of course, have the problem of flipping irretrievably, but also are liable to remain afloat as an upside down raft.

A lot of forethought, ingenuity and perhaps cash should go into the solution of this problem. Finding the money for a long voyage is generally a vexatious task. I was extremely lucky in my ventures to have sponsorship from a newspaper, the *Daily Express*, from Rank Films and from ITV. Some people have been able to do it on a shoestring and a sabbatical year off. Someone posed for me the idea of a 'Brave New World'. You work hard until the age of, say, thirty-five or forty; everyone is then laid off for a spell of sport, adventure or fun. Instead of retiring at sixty-five you re-enter the rat race, regenerated by your experiences, and substitute a new career for the boredom of old age. It may, I fear, never happen, nor my own scheme for vastly extended sea-adventure opportunity for young people; but what shall we do when industry is totally robotized?

MEDICAL AND SURGICAL

I have had absolutely no training in medicine or surgery or any field of health care, but was entirely responsible in these fields for submarine crews at sea during the Second World War.

My overall experience is that in the medical field, if someone fell sick he would be put to bed, given reassurance, and would recover. Furthermore, I found that those in responsible positions did not go sick on war patrol: has the body some inner responsibility? When incipient scurvy struck, men who suffered were those in least responsible positions; in this connection it must be observed, all had the same food.

Surgery is, of course, quite another matter and I am surgically squeamish as well as ignorant. In the earlier part of the war, when we were busy losing it or just hanging on, I steeled myself to the fact that if anyone got mashed up we could not leave patrol. They would have to die or suffer our rude surgery.

Later, in the Pacific, when there were battle wounds, I was relieved to find that my second-in-command was the son of a doctor and had experience in his father's surgery. Later still, when someone suffered a bad accident, I judged the war to be almost over and withdrew from the front line to transfer my suffering casualty to a flying boat.

Now to relate this experience to that of an ocean-crossing lone sailor. I found that once again I never went sick and my medicine chest contained only Elastoplast and a tooth repair outfit with which I was able to replace a filling which had come out.

After reading the experiences of Dr David Lewis, who used antibiotics and painkillers in a case of frostbite, I think one should perhaps consult an expert on what to take as a pharmacopoeia? Surgery again is a troublesome subject; the problem of dealing with one's own fearsome injury does make the mind boggle.

One has, of course, an endless supply of that excellent disinfectant, salt water, but bone fractures may require splints and Lewis mentions inflatable splints which must be something new. Cold water is the latest specific for burns. I have heard that it is best applied on clean, sterile linen laid on the wound. I would think that sea water would do, so long as it is not polluted. To sum up, it would probably be wise to consult some friendly expert, someone perhaps who knew any personal problems which you might have, to advise on what equipment and other measures to take. Above all do not worry about a subject which is a frequent cause of worry.

CHAPTER TWELVE

Home is the Sailor

Between two lone voyages I flew back from Australia across the Pacific with my wife. We stopped at Samoa for a nostalgic visit. My wife's American grandfather, Henry Clay Ide, had been Chief Justice of the island. During his term of office his family became close friends of Robert Louis Stevenson. Ide's daughter Anne, who was living with them, had been born at Christmas and suffered therefore, by duplication, from a dearth of presents. Robert Louis Stevenson made a will, in romantic terms, bequeathing his birthday, a mid-year event, to the deprived girl. The will was ratified by Congress and signed by the President of the USA.

We climbed along a winding jungle path to the summit of the hill where the writer is buried. On his gravestone is inscribed his famous couplet:

> Home is the sailor, home from sea,
> And the hunter home from the hill.

The lines ring for me, and so I will digress into the field of fox-hunting which dates back to our remote ancestry.

There is a small vociferous group which opposes fox-hunting; ostensibly on the grounds that by abolishing it we should make the world a happier place for foxes. Foxes are, however, predators on fowl and new-born lambs and farmers will always control their numbers with traps, guns and poison, all of which frequently result in lingering deaths.

The chase and quick kill are far more humane. But what is there in it for the followers? At a recent dinner party in the house of a distinguished single-handed yachtsman, not an equestrian, our host put a question to one of his guests, an Irish lady well known in the hunting field. 'What is the attraction?' he asked. 'It is hard to say,' she replied. 'For a start you are always terrified.' I also gave a start. I had always thought that I was the only one who was terrified. Well, of course, it is an adventure to ride a long hunt in the wake of a fast pack of hounds across, say, County Galway, when you may jump two hundred walls in the course of a day. This brings me back to the concept of the similarity of the adventurous life of the ancient hunters and the modern lone sailor. The hunter returned to his cave. The sailor finally comes back to harbour.

The astonishing fact is that as a lone voyager one can transmute at once into the world of human beings from which one has been separated for many months – a loving family, a circle of friends or just a welcoming concourse. Perhaps the very fact that one has been on a long 'retreat' has reactivated the magnets of human contact.

Shortly after I returned from a long voyage, a friend, who is very perceptive, said to me, 'Your soul is in very good order.' Well, perhaps it should have been; for a long time one had not been able to do, in general, those things which one ought not to have done, nor to leave undone those things which one ought to have done. One has simply plugged along; but you can scarcely do that for ever.

The most notable thing about one's return to the human race after a long solo voyage is the immediacy. It is as though you have never been away. I wonder perhaps if, as many people believe, we reunite after death with our family and friends who have predeceased us, the same sort of situation might then occur. My first landfall, unscheduled in 1970 was in Cape Town, my boat dismasted and limping. The outsider's impression of South Africa is of sjambok-wielding Boers and furious blacks burning their political opponents to death. At this time, however, I met numbers of smiling friendly people of all races.

Possibly I was able to step over the divide, being at that time sunburned blacker than many of the coloured folk. But, of course, there were already rumblings of discontent in those days and one broadminded observer said to me, 'It is sad that the blacks and whites will fight over this lovely land. Of course, it should really belong to the yellow original habitants, the Bushmen and Hottentots, but they were largely exterminated.'

This made me hark back to my own fatherland, Ireland, where

Irish Catholic Celts and re-entered Scottish Protestant Celts are in ancient dispute. The British, Britannic, Pretannic or Pictish Isles belong, if there is such as thing as belong, to the ancient Picts. There remain, I once read, five words of their language, and the record of the Roman soldiers on Hadrian's Wall looking in wonderment at the painted body of a dead Pict. Well, they were small and had pointed faces. So am I, but I won't make an individual claim to those islands.

On several occasions I have had to enter coastal waters and harbours on unintended entry without benefit of the local charts. This was, of course, the lot of early explorers, but in my case, as an experienced mariner, I had the benefit of the memory of previous voyages. Nosing up towards Fremantle, Western Australia, I recalled the times when I had returned there in my submarine after long patrols in the Pacific and Java Sea. The warmhearted Australian welcome released the tensions of groping in tropic waters close to the palm trees off the coast of Malaya under constant attention from Japanese coastal defence forces. The words 'pommie bastards' were a term of endearment. Twenty-six years later I could remember the entry north of Rottnest Island which guards Gage Roads and Cockburn Sound, off the port of Fremantle. As *Galway Blazer II* approached in somewhat hazy weather I was alarmed to see a cathedral growing out of the sea where, I distinctly remembered, there had not been one before. It started me taking new rounds of cross bearings and leaping down below to check my last sights and latest position. It took quite a long time for the penny to drop and for me to realize that an oil rig was moored in the place where my submarine used to exchange recognition signals with the shore station.

My Australian welcome was just as heartwarming as had been my wartime returnings. On the jetty was the wife of my late skipper, John Illingworth, last seen at the finish of a Bermuda Race. New-found friends took me into their homes as one of the family, old friendships were renewed, a member of my submarine's crew turned up: he had married locally and was now a successful businessman.

In Australia there is plenty of room, and people do not, as in England, keep their elbows close to their sides, which is an indication of population pressure.

I had an embarrassment of riches from invitations from the Royal Perth and Royal Freshwater Bay Yacht Clubs, to berth and refurbish my boat. I had to take the first one received, the RFBYC whose shipwright supervized my breathtaking entry into the Swan River. The road and rail bridges across the river were built too low to accommodate any mast higher than that of a dinghy. A plan was evolved to heel the boat 46° to clear the mast for the tow. Oildrums filled with water were lashed to the deck; on the same side sat the heaviest members of the yacht club. The last few degrees were achieved by hauling down the mastheads by tackles to the towing launch alongside. As we shot under the bridges the aluminium supports for the masthead windvanes clicked on the bottom of the bridge girders. My heart stopped clicking, in case we repeated the dismasting by the hurricane, something for which I had no funds to repair.

I have particularly warm memories of Marko, the owner and manager of the boat repair yard in Fremantle. He had a limp from some terrible leg injury of which he made light, moving round the boats in agile fashion and encouraging his men in Italian, Serbo-Croat and Australian. When my boat returned to Fremantle with a large jagged hole inflicted by an undersea attacker, reaching below the waterline, Marko produced a young Seychellois expert who made an impeccable repair, which should have cost over a thousand pounds.

On receiving a bill for fifty pounds I said, 'Marko, you will never be a millionaire!' 'Friendship is more important' he replied.

Much of my early life was centred in the West Country of England: schooling, submarine flotillas based on Devonport, and here, into Plymouth Sound I returned from Australia in my submarine at the end of six years of war, then to find myself in the grip of a frightful anticlimax; the outbreak of peace was too sudden. In May 1972, *Galway Blazer II* was approaching the Devon coast. Visibility was clear out to seaward and I was able to take a longitude sight and home in along the position line more or less at right angles to the coast; a classic approach as there was dense mist over the shoreline.

The first thing I saw was Plymouth Breakwater, a few feet above the sea. Here I experienced absolutely no anticlimax. My loving family and friends came out to meet me, in boats. The chief of staff to the Naval Commander-in-Chief stepped nimbly on board and helped me to berth; I observed that post captains seemed to be getting younger and the Commander-in-Chief was the *son* of an admiral under whom I once served. Among the welcomers was Admiral Ruck-Keene who had been my flotilla captain during much of the war. We were entertained in the home of a submarine flotilla captain. To me it was as if I had never been away, but, of course, life has to be taken up again, paid for in cash, organized in sequence, and foreplanned. Somewhere over the horizon are my remote ancestors living with nature. I have left them for a while.

CHAPTER THIRTEEN

The Lone Sailor – Never Alone

Notwithstanding a commonly held misconception, no two people are exactly alike, in temperament, physique or metabolism. Physiological differences apart, women can be measured by the same standards as men. Human survivability hinges on these facts. Isolation can accentuate these differences in progressive stages – from strong individualism to eccentricity and finally insanity; the last, if not due to brain damage, may well be simply a retreat from an unpleasant reality.

I recall the commanding officer of a wartime submarine flotilla noting with resigned disapproval the strong individualism of his submarine captains, making it difficult to enforce a common policy. I pictured myself as disciplined and conventional – a picture which faded with time.

For the final campaign of the war in 1944/45 I took over command of a new type of submarine, HMS *Telemachus*, embodying various modifications. Her bridge had been altered by cutting off the frontal cab, which in previous designs had sheltered the forward part of the platform.

As we were intended to operate in the warm area of the Pacific Ocean, I had planned to sleep, when on the surface at night, on the little brass chart table on the bridge, in order to be able to make an instant response to enemy action: but there was no overhead shelter to protect me from showers, spray or dew. On our eastward passage we had to dwell a pause in Port Said. I persuaded the Suez Canal Company's excellent dockyard to rebuild the bridge cab just as it had been in previous designs. I had reason to be very glad of my decision when we were surprised by a Japanese attacker on a dark night and I was ready at the command post.

On return to Devonport dockyard when war ended I heard some

baffled mutterings from people who were certain that *Telemachus* had been launched with an open bridge. In the confusion of peace breaking out, my individualism was never officially questioned.

Further along the scale is eccentricity and this flourishes in isolated societies and was prominent among the now defunct Anglo-Irish Protestant 'ascendancy', cut off from the vast majority of their fellow countrymen by race, affluence, tradition, culture and religion.

One noble lord of vast wealth used to live alone in his kitchen on tea and biscuits. I remember when my wife and I with a guest invaded his household he reluctantly shared his frugal meal with us, but there was one chocolate biscuit on the plate over which he kept his hand in case someone might select it.

My wife recounted that at one time her family home in County Monaghan was teetotal in that no drink was offered to family or guests. The squire, however, had a bottle of excellent claret beside his plate for his own consumption.

The stories are endless and most of them apocryphal, but the wealth of them points to the eccentricity bred of isolation.

Serving in the China Fleet in the early 1930s I heard tales of eccentric commanding officers of the river gunboats, divided from their peers by a thousand miles of Yangtse Kiang. These boats navigated in very shallow water. One of the captains made his coxswain wade ahead of the ship wearing red bathing drawers: when the red pants appeared above the surface of the river, it was time to alter course. More conventional people used a sounding pole up in the bows of the ship.

Eccentricity may lead to insanity. I remember hearing a psychiatrist broadcast on radio a plea to the general public to be understanding of schizophrenics and other such sufferers. He seemed to be telling us that we all have traces of split personality, that all of us are in varying degrees inclined to be manic depressive.

So where does the lone sailor fit into the pattern which I have woven, of difference, individuality, eccentricity, or insanity? From my own experience I think that one probably travels up and down the scale.

One cannot be entirely normal to contemplate such a mode of life; certainly eccentricity showed in my choice of diet. From time to time,

I probably went a bit dotty: dotty, that is, compared with one's normal self when simply working the ship.

It has to be remembered that two contestants in the single-handed non-stop round-the-world race of 1969 committed suicide.

When rounding Cape Horn during an extended period of exceptionally bad weather, I had the hallucination that someone else was there. Once when down below calculating on the chart, I thought that the other chap was looking out; once hammering in some wedges I thought that he was sleeping below and that I ought not to wake him. I certainly did not then envisage some form of divine intervention, but I suppose that as the going was very tough I must have felt a strong desire that there should be someone around to help and that my mind went over the edge of normality by providing for a helper, but only for a very short space of time.

This sort of thing does happen to mountaineers and polar explorers, strangely enough to those who do have companions: possibly extreme hardship imposes a sense of being alone. During my struggle to keep the boat afloat after being holed by a shark I had no such hallucination. This was a time of ceaseless mental and physical activity.

Having excessively low blood pressure I came to realize that a person in this condition should not be messing about in the vicinity of Antarctica. I found out, the hard way, that the skin of my hands would not stand up to constant immersion in cold water: the skin just peeled off and this had caused me to break off, into Western Australia, what was intended to be a non-stop circumnavigation. On my final voyage I combated my disability by carrying a locker full of surgeon's heavy-duty rubber gloves and by judicious use of these I got through the cold-water belt, but only just. On several occasions I was on the point of turning north for warmer water to return home by the Panama Canal.

There was a line in a prayer used in services on board ships of the Royal Navy which read: 'Preserve us, o Lord, from the dangers of the sea and from the violence of the enemy.' During six years of submarine warfare, with the constant realization that one was unlikely to survive, although being a conventionally religious person, I never reached for my prayer book. Perhaps I felt that I was not leading the sort of life which entitled me to divine assistance.

A long period of indecision about the continuation of my lone sailing voyage with hands deteriorating in spite of my precautions, brought me to the New Testament which I had read from cover to cover. I noted in St Mark's Gospel, Chapter 11, verse 25, the words of Christ: 'And whenever you stand praying, forgive, if you have anything against any one; so that your Father also who is in heaven may forgive you your trespasses.'

The next verse read: 'and forgive not with your lips but in your heart.' Like most people I do have 'those against whom I have something', and the whole operation sounded jolly difficult; but I felt impelled to try it out, and jolly difficult it was. I prayed in this fashion that I might continue with my intended voyage and at some point I decided to hold the course for Cape Horn.

But when I re-read the Gospel that second verse was *not there*, nor have I been able to find it anywhere else. If there is an interpretation of this it must be left to the theologians or psychiatrists: one must be a little mad to invent a piece of New Testament.

This experience, if it can be believed, poses the question, 'Was there an answer to prayer?' and I think 'yes', possibly if it did so by increasing my own effort. What happened after the voyage is, of course, an example of human frailty: when I got ashore, the 'anything against' factor crept slowly back.

In a hypothetical case that there could be, for me, a re-run of the last war, would I, with total hindsight, pray to be preserved from the violence of the enemy? In that mighty struggle we appeared to be fighting against evil, the monstrous regime of the National Socialist Party and the brutality of Japanese militarism. None the less we fought *for* Stalin and Soviet socialism. I have met one or two survivors of his Gulags. The only difference from the German extermination camps was that in the evenings tipper lorries arrived. The dead and dying were loaded up and dumped in the forests: they froze in winter and the wolves ate them in summer. In crowded Germany there was a sanitary problem, so they had to be incinerated.

In Homer's *Iliad* the ebb and flow of battles were ascribed to the intervention of gods or goddesses on the side of their choice, certainly a good excuse for defeat. In the hypothetical case which I was considering, I should, I think opt to pray for deliverance from the dangers of the sea and leave the issue of battle to fate. The eruption of war was in any case the fault of woolly-minded democracies who let down their defences in the face of ruthless powerful dictatorships: a clear case of the operation of Murphy's Third Law. We were simply fighting for our lives.

Another question which I have been asked was 'Did your voyage make you think about your religion and would you wish to change your faith?' The answer is no I would not. I was brought up in the Protestant Church of England faith. In my early days the unspoken prayer was said to be 'God bless the squire and his relations and keep us in our proper stations.' Now in the late 1980s it seems to have gone trendy lefty. I don't take either of those aberrations very seriously: there are plenty of splendid pastors doing their job, teaching the word of God, preaching the imitation of Christ, of which most of us make a very poor replica. I noticed that, at the time and in the country where Christ preached there were gross inequalities of wealth, barbarous judicial punishments, slavery and military occupation by a foreign power. Against none of these social evils did Christ inveigh: his message was to the individual alone.

My complete reading of the New Testament with plenty of time to consider it confirmed me in my beliefs and doctrines. My impression, formed from reading the accounts of other lone sailors, is that the experience of an enlargement of faith is fairly general.

CHAPTER FOURTEEN

La Belle France

When Britain first, at Heaven's command,
Arose from out the azure main.

I can never find the script, but I think that those are the opening bars of that stirring ditty 'Rule Britannia', of which the chorus never fails to evoke for me the memory and imagination of the crash of broadsides. In 1927, as a naval cadet perched in the fighting top of HMS Nelson, I heard the thunder and saw the flash of nine 16-inch guns being fired on their first trials. Fifteen years later those same guns pounded the *Bismarck* into impotence. A few more bars from 'Rule Britannia' and I can hear the ripple of the *Victory*'s cannon at Trafalgar.

I remember seeing a cartoon of the seated Britannia, resembling an amalgam of Queen Victoria and a sea goddess, rising slowly from the waves. But of course we know scientifically that it was not so. A subsidence of bridging land, an irruption of the sea and a peninsula on the western edge of Northern Europe became the sceptred isle whose people, after a few successful invasions of their country, learned about the importance of sea power.

The islanders were amazingly fortunate in two ways: the sea gave them immunity from sudden attacks by land and the island, being to the westward, was generally upwind of their European rivals in the days when the square-rigged fighting ships were poor performers to windward. Also the island largely closed off the exits from the German Ocean or North Sea. Growing out of this was a steadily increasing supremacy at sea culminating in the vast British maritime empire by which so much of the globe was coloured red in my youth. Perhaps the very fact of the dissolution of that empire should induce those in

Britain to look with a more friendly eye at their neighbours. Only today someone remarked to me: 'What do we want with the Channel Tunnel? The French and ourselves detest each other.' I don't think that we should – especially those of us who sail.

Popular feeding habits are closely linked with the emotions; and the extent of this can be gauged from the fact that derogatory remarks, intended insults, aimed at rival nations, are based upon typical articles of their diet. In anglophone countries the Germans are known as 'krauts', from their habit of ensiling cabbage for sauerkraut; this may well be one of the sources of their strength, but to the English imagination, cabbage exists as they themselves serve it: overcooked, nasty and smelly. Similarly, the Italians were at one time known as 'icecreams', eaters of children's fare. The French are called 'frogs', for they actually eat the nasty slimy creatures, used by practical jokers to put in unsuspecting people's beds. The British are still called 'limeys' or 'rosbifs'. The Navy always refer to West Countrymen as 'oggies' after their Cornish pasties. (Full name tiddy oggies.) Scots are 'haggis', and anyone born into a Murphy family is 'Spud'.

Over many centuries, staccato attempts have been made to bridge the emotional gap which corresponds to the English Channel: for instance, Henry VIII at the Field of the Cloth of Gold, Edward VII with the Entente Cordiale and Winston Churchill's offer of common citizenship while France was being engulfed by fast-moving panzer divisions. Nothing very much came of all these, but with the advent of a true Common Market and the Channel Tunnel forecast to be open for business in 1993, there is a need for an increase in understanding above and beyond the evolution of Franglais, which is in any case held in equal detestation by the French with that of the English for a French bus queue, fought out with sharpened elbows.

People of Irish, Scottish and Welsh descent have considerable affinity with France, stemming from the racial ties between Gael and Gaul: perhaps for this reason I became a francophile in early life; perhaps also because, during a school holiday in France I ate frogs' legs, *cuisses de grenouilles*, cooked in garlic and butter, and found them to be utterly delicious.

My wife, an Irish Catholic, admired the spirit and chic of France. She had been a student in Paris, and in 1944 enlisted in the French First Army as an ambulance driver and rode the crest of the advance from Marseilles to Alsace, finishing up in Berlin in Hitler's bunker, and bringing home the Croix de Guerre, awarded on the field of battle for rescuing the wounded under heavy fire. Her cousin, Winston Churchill, used her as a sounding-board for French opinion.

To achieve an understanding it is necessary to know the national differences. The French have an unashamed attachment to glory; the English reaction to glory is one of embarrassment. 'He put up quite a good show' means to say that he had won a VC, commanded at some famous victory or had an Olympic gold medal. The French habit of smoking ostentatiously in non-smoking areas stems perhaps from their individuality, and to defy has a touch of glory.

Also, the British in fortunate insular security should understand the appalling trauma caused by the defeat of France in 1940 and the five years of occupation and domination by Germany under the brutal rule of the National Socialist Party, followed by the ravages of the counter invasion of 1944 when France became a battlefield. For our part we have too readily accepted the myth that the British Expeditionary Force in 1940 was doomed by the collapse of further effective resistance by Belgian and French troops on either flank. The fact is that there was considerable heroic resistance against hopeless odds even after the miracle of the evacuation from Dunkirk was over. For example, the 1,000 officer cadets of the French cavalry school at Saumur on the Loire held out for three vital days in June against 10,000 panzer troops.

After VE-Day the painstaking rebuilding of their shattered cities was an outward and visible sign of the resurgence of a great nation healing its terrible internal wounds. Colonel Blondie Hasler, who led the Royal Marines' raid on Bordeaux in folboats (later filmed as *Cockleshell Heroes*) returned in early post-war years to cruise along the French coast. He recounted to me the astonishing verve, energy and enthusiasm of a whole new generation of French sailors.

It is surely not too fanciful to link this, partly in cause and partly in effect, with their national recovery after the humiliation of 1940.

The French look for heroes, and a popular national hero arose in the person of Eric Tabarly, a young regular naval officer from Brittany who was also a superb seaman. I met him briefly at some function: charming and unassuming, he radiated strength and competence. Realizing his potential, the French Navy seconded Tabarly to the sport of ocean racing and French industry backed him financially. Tabarly and others inspired largely by him, excelled in competitive ocean sailing, both solo and with crews, in a field which, an exultant French press noted, 'the Anglo-Saxons had regarded as their own'. I recall, however, at a very convivial dinner celebrating the finish of a Fastnet Race, that the admiral of the club completed his speech with these telling words: 'Ocean racing is not international, it is cosmopolitan.' Ardent competition should take second place to warm friendly contact – through a common interest.

It is not my brief to chronicle the many notable voyages of lone sailors from Slocum onwards. This has already been done with great thoroughness and virtuosity by D. H. Clarke in *An Evolution of Single Handers* (Stanford Marine, London). Nor do I intend to bring his record further up to date. Most of the successful voyagers are well known and documented in their own countries and internationally. As usual, however, I will depart a little from my intention.

Following in the wake of Tabarly, his pupil and collaborator, Alain Colas, sailed into a meteoric career. He purchased Tabarly's trimaran *Pen Duick IV* which, to me, resembled a spacecraft and, after sailing her to victory in the OSTAR of 1972, renamed her *Manureva* and accompanied the Whitbread Round-the-World Race for monohulls, achieving a record passage for the course. Like a depressing number of solo multihull sailors, Colas was finally lost at sea without trace in the French 'Route du Rhum' single-handed race to the Caribbean.

'*Tant va la crûche à l'eau, qu'à la fin elle se casse*' – 'The pitcher goes once too often to the well'. Also remember a multihull which flips, stays flipped – a monohull comes upright.

So now to a monohull and one of the most astonishing feats on record – Marcel Bardiaux in *Les 4 Vents*. Bardiaux, unlike me, was a complete professional, ironmaster, fitter, welder, mechanic, painter and electrician. He built his own boat, a traditional long-keeled sloop of overall length 9.19 metres whose displacement was 4 tons. He sailed a long circumnavigational cruise, lasting eight years and stopping off in many places. He sailed the Roaring Forties against the prevailing westerly wind, rounding Cape Horn in that direction in *winter*, experiencing temperatures of −27°C. I cannot conceive of this sort of possibility. I recall my hands going dead driving an open tractor on a fine but breezy summer evening in Galway. So, a salute from me to

Bardiaux, a salute to France, especially to her mariners, Gerbault, Marin Marie, Tabarly, Colas, Moitessier, Le Toumelin, Bardiaux, Jeantot and all others who sailed or will sail in their wake. Do not despise the search for glory for therein you may find yourself. Let us establish an '*entente des marins*' and exclude acrimony and yobbism from a sport which is essentially participatory.

CHAPTER FIFTEEN

Portrait of a Loner: Francis Chichester and Others

There is a widely-held tradition that religion, politics and shop should be excluded from conversation at social occasions: the two former subjects generate heat, the latter boredom. This is perhaps in general a wise rule, but rules were made for fools and for the guidance of wise people. I believe that in an intelligent civilized society there should be no taboos. Taboo is the hallmark of savage man.

At a very pleasant dinner party in the house of Sir Francis and Lady Chichester in the winter before his final voyage there was, besides myself, a mixed gathering. One of the guests was a dedicated left-winger, perhaps in the vein of Mao-Tse-tung, not then a fallen idol. There was at the time a miners' strike in progress and the subject was discussed among us in a balanced manner. Francis was, I think, conservative in his outlook. The left-wing person, who naturally supported the miners, exclaimed, 'But you don't know what it is like to be a miner.' Francis replied mildly 'Well, as a matter of fact, I have been a miner', exhibiting some of those blue scars which are the hallmark of that trade.

Francis had experienced an unusually unhappy childhood. He grew up in a Christian household (his father was a Church of England parson) which, for him, lacked the one really essential ingredient of Christianity – love. This insecurity must have ill-fitted him for the next segment of the life of an English upper-class boy, preparatory and public boarding schools: the regime being dominated by relentless flogging, a form of licensed sadism, and bullying. Finally he managed to drop out before the end of the stint and as a non-inheriting scion of the squirearchy he was faced with the only three possible alternatives, the services, the Church or – for those unsuitable for these pursuits – the colonies.

Francis had poor eyesight and must have had his fill of religion. He went to New Zealand and became in turn farmworker, miner and gold prospector. The fact that, being a member of a large and powerful North Devon land-owning clan, he threw himself with energy and enthusiasm into manual work with heavy labour, indicated his determination to make his own way. Finally he made his way into business from the bottom, touting as a door-to-door salesman and, in spite of the world slump of 1929 and onwards, made enough money, but only just enough, to embark on his career of the adventure which his aggressive spirit required.

In my view, his early achievements in long-distance solo flying surpassed his later, more publicized, lone sailing feats.

Francis was a perfectionist, a state of mind which I can well understand, being one myself, but unlike me, and I think probably a large number of others similarly afflicted, he was a perfectionist who could get it together, and this requires clarity of purpose, dedication and determination. It was said of Arthur Wellesley, Duke of Wellington, that he went to the point of action, saw what had to be done and did it. Most of us don't. Strong characters are, I suppose, mostly ingrained but also possibly partly forged by coping with early difficulties.

Francis trained himself to be an excellent pilot of an aircraft and superb navigator. He was a slow learner because, being a perfectionist, he was not content to know that certain things happened: he wanted to know *why* they happened. Most teachers and manuals don't tell us this. Amy Johnson, one of the most distinguished early lone fliers, said that Francis was the greatest navigator in the world, and in this connection I think that his crossing of the Tasman Sea in a small open-cockpit *Gipsy Moth* aircraft, with no radio aids, surpassed even his lone flight to Australia from Britain. His tiny plane, which had been converted into a seaplane for the flight, had a limited range and could only make the flight by leapfrogging across the sea, alighting at two tiny islands. The experts said that it was impossible.

I know from experience some of the difficulties involved. In 1928 I was undergoing a short course in aeronautics with the Fleet Air Arm. Having discovered that my talent as a pilot was minimal, I went out on an exercise as observer/navigator. Our mission accomplished, the problem was to rediscover the carrier. The course and speed of our aircraft, the carrier and the wind had to be calculated and vectored. By the time I had the sum completed we had gone so far that it was time to work out another velocity triangle. The experience was similar to the occasion when, in a boxing tournament, I found myself fighting a professional.

Francis's feat was this. As the aircraft bubble sextant was not sufficiently accurate, he taught himself to come down low over the sea and take sights with a marine-type sextant, chasing the sun through clouds, and work them out on his kneepad with the engine roaring in his ears and the wind whistling past. This was equivalent to playing a complicated concerto with one hand and one half of one's brain while the other halves played a match in first-class tennis.

In 1931, Francis started to fly his *Gipsy Moth* alone round the world, an attempt which ended in disaster in Japan. He was asked to perform a demonstration flight round a harbour, but had not been forewarned of a high telephone cable into which the plane crashed and fell to earth. The plane was a write-off; Francis almost was. I think that the terrible injuries and trauma probably largely contributed to the cancer which plagued his post-war life.

Francis had an early failed marriage and was shy and awkward with girls. This is normal in a man whose life has been physical, hard labour and adventure. Aptitude in this sphere belongs to those whose life is social or bohemian. In 1936 Francis met, took by storm and married the next year Sheila Craven, artistic and sophisticated – his opposite. Their one common attribute was being penniless members of rich and powerful families. Her cousin, Sir Charles Craven, whom I knew, had been a submariner in the First World War, retired from the Navy and got a job at Barrow-in-Furness with Vickers, who built submarines. He rose to be chairman of the company and had the rare distinction of being a captain of industry who inspired devotion in his workforce. Sheila supported and looked after Francis with a similar dedication to that shown by Clementine Churchill with her difficult Winston. Francis was very fortunate to have this support through thick and thin: there was to be a lot of thin.

The war years were spent in utter frustration. His talents were needed by the RAF in navigational instruction – but owing to his poor eyesight he was never allowed to fly operationally: to one of his expertise and audacity this was a continuing gall.

After the war he inducted himself into the sailing and ocean racing world; but between this period and his well-documented lone-sailing feats he was stricken with lung cancer. It was decided that one lung should be removed and he was resigned to this. Sheila, however, insisted that recourse to nature cure, prayer and faith would cure the symptoms – and so they did. What courage!

Francis had the reward of the very great navigator – the extra touch which told him of unsuspected danger – the heightened awareness of where he actually was in poor visibility. The Revd. Stephen Pakenham, who sailed in one of the OSTARs, told me that he felt that the competitors seemed to gain a knowledge of longitude as they crossed the foggy Newfoundland Banks. He told me of lugworms who navigated in three dimensions by metal molecules in whatever they have as brains, tuned to the earth's magnetic field. I have noticed that if you dig up an earthworm and throw it to another part of the garden to save it from injury, the blind creature streaks straight back to where it was disinterred. If worms can do it, so perhaps can we.

Further, Francis looked upon his sea voyages as health cures. This idea is paralleled for me by my experience of another great sailing friend, Bobby Somerset. Bobby told me that he had, all his youth, a mysterious recurring illness which no one could diagnose or cure. Finally he cured it by embarking and working in a North Sea herring trawler. He spent his post-war life mostly afloat and also once said to me, 'I don't really like being ashore. I never feel well there.'

To digress somewhat, Bobby, one of the most enchanting sailing companions, served in both world wars in all three services – land, air and sea. In the First World War as a young officer in the Coldstream Guards he won a DSO for an action which Lord Digby, his CO at the time, later told me was worth a VC. After the war he was awarded a gold watch by President Roosevelt and the Blue Water Medal of the Cruising Club of America for saving the crew of the American yacht *Adriana* which had caught fire during the Bermuda Race. Finally he was drowned trying to save life at sea; greater love hath no man.

Before we say farewell to Francis here is one more tribute to a great navigator.

There is a method of determining longitude if the correct time is not known. It is achieved by observation of the moon. I think Slocum knew it. I don't know it – Francis did. He published in the *Journal of the Institute of Navigation* an elegant method of determining longitude at sea without reference to Greenwich Mean Time.

At a press interview shortly before his death Francis put all adventure in a nutshell: 'Life is dull without a challenge, but don't just go pothunting. If your try fails, what does that matter – all life is a failure in the end. The thing is to get sport out of trying.'

Someone wrote, 'After Chichester there could be no further interest in lone sailing, unless you were royalty or a dog.' I had a mental picture of a corgi, sailing single-pawed round Cape Horn, waving the other paw, in royal fashion, at circling aircraft.

But after Chichester interest in single-handed off-shore sailing redoubled. Robin Knox-Johnston sailed to victory as the only finisher in the Round-the-World Race of 1969/70 and was the first to circle the globe non-stop. His boat *Suhaili* had been built in India by craftsmen with adzes. Sailed home to UK she had a lot of wear and Robin had a great deal of difficulty, including patching a leak *under water* in the tropics. I took his book recounting the voyage to sea with me to encourage me during my voyage round Cape Horn.

I had very great admiration for Robin's feat of circumnavigation – more so for his chivalrous act in awarding his prize money to the widow of the unfortunate suicide Donald Crowhurst – a victim of loneliness I think. A true gentleman is one who considers others before himself. Consider the difference between this act and the squabbling stars in other fields of sport, and remember that the Single-handed Transatlantic Race was initiated by Blondie Hasler and Francis Chichester for a wager of half-a-crown – little over 20 pence.

CHAPTER SIXTEEN

Farewell

While bidding you farewell I propose to make an imaginative forecast of another extended voyage.

Owing to a late marriage and my reluctance to leave my children until they had grown up, my circumnavigational voyage was postponed until I was in my sixties. Now, being nearly eighty, I have young grandchildren and, although I am sure they do not notice if I am there, I do not feel like leaving them, at present; so my next turn around Cape Horn will have to wait until I am ninety. For this plan there are two requirements: I must hurry up and make my first million to be able to afford a boat of suitable design, also to plan for a boat which will take a nonagenarian round Cape Horn. This plan summarizes much of what I have written earlier.

The dream boat will keep the essential design of *Galway Blazer II*, a whale-backed deck, no guard rails, long end, spoon bow, high freeboard with tumblehome.

The modifications will be aimed at preventing a recurrence of my capsize and rollover and to take advantage of modern technology and materials: and of course the latter will probably improve further between now and the actual project.

When discussing the original hull formation with the designer, Angus Primrose, I specified a traditional long keel because I believed it would run more steadily on long ocean passages. My first *Galway Blazer*, a small ocean cruiser/racer, had a short fin keel, but for the transatlantic passage I had fitted removable extensions fore and aft. With the removal of a few bolts the staid ocean-crosser became a lively ocean racer.

Angus, however, talked me out of the long keel. He argued that a short-keeled lively boat would be easier on the vane steering. I now think that there would have been an additional advantage to the long keel: it can carry the ballast, distributed along its length, with shallower draft than a fin keel and thus, if hurled sideways down the face of a wave, would not reach so far into the central, more static part of the wave and thus be less likely to trip the boat. I notice that Bardiaux's boat had a long keel drawing only 4 foot 9 inches.

The next thing to consider is how to reduce the capsizing moment due to heavy tophamper. The masts could be made considerably lighter by using carbon fibre, as also the heavy full-length sail battens which were then of hickory. Perhaps the most important device would be a modern vane steering equipment which would keep going in hurricane-force winds. Thus you could run on downwind and not heave to dead in the water.

But in this connection I should also like a sail designer to evolve a method of heaving to in a junk so that she would not lie ahull but fore-reach slowly. I visualize a mini-try-sail of very small area and very high-aspect ratio hoisted on the mainmast and fastened to the mast by detachable parrels: the sail area should be minute to take hurricane-force winds, but just enough to influence the boat into luffing a little above the beam-on position and fore-reaching. The inbuilt bipod jury mast would of course be retained.

Now what about the scantlings and material of the hull? I am very much wedded to the idea of the light displacement hull which has the ability to 'roll with the punches'. None the less I was impressed by the fact that the impact of the whale that hit *Ghostwing* off Portugal in 1982 was very much like the blow of the shark which stove in *Galway Blazer II* ten years earlier. *Ghostwing* was somewhat damaged, but the fibreglass hull was not breached. I told the owner that I would never again call his boat *Tupperware*. *Ghostwing* was of heavier scantlings than *Galway Blazer*, about 12 tons displacement on 40 feet overall as against *Galway Blazer*'s 4½ tons on 42 feet. I discussed this matter with Leslie Powles, who said, 'With modern materials you might have the best of both worlds.' Well, by the time I am ninety the materials should be further improved – perhaps an indestructible microlite.

The decision on what 'high-technology' equipment to take will have to wait – the shopping-list must be made in the light of further developments, but the guiding principles are:

1   No propulsive engine and hopefully no battery-charging motor.
2   Battery chargers powered by wind, water and solar panels.
3   A press-button navigator.
4   An ultra-bright masthead light.
5   A radar signal receiver.
6   The latest automatic SOS unit.
· 7   A solar still for fresh water.

Yes, I shall need that million, but I won't have heads – 'bucket-and-chuck-it'.

The rig will remain substantially the same – fully battened junk sails. However, I have spotted a brilliant innovation. In August 1983, two Frenchmen, Lucien Burquier and Jean-Michel Raynard, sailed their single-masted junk *Lucretia* into Galway Bay. The forward ends of the sail battens, instead of lying against the mast, had their forward ends split, doubled and formed into parrels which encircled the mast, the sail being also doubled to cover them round the mast. The parrels did not touch the mast, but there were internal bearing surfaces of rope covered with a strong material with a low coefficient of friction and lubricated. The whole outfit appeared to be a great improvement both for handling and windward efficiency. We went for a sail across Galway Bay and then sat on our lawn drinking wine and discussing the junk rig with a visiting lady master of foxhounds. The two Frenchmen were intending to make an ocean voyage and I should love to know how they got on.

To conclude, I shall again depart from my intention not to chronicle solo voyages and report on one of the finest examples of triumph over difficulty which I have ever come across.

Leslie Powles in *Solitaire* was the first to sail single-handed non-stop south of the Five Capes. He sailed from Lymington (UK) back to Lymington causing a problem to the customs officer – how could he return after 329 days at sea without going somewhere? Actually, far from carrying dutiable goods he had run out of food!

Leslie, an excellent craftsman but unpractised in seamanship and navigation and with no financial resources, built his own boat and sailed, on what turned out to be a training run, on a circumnavigation through the warm, well, mostly warm, route using the Panama Canal. He ran into many disasters, including a thousand-mile error in position. He used his experience gained to sail the 'impossible route' and round Cape Horn. In the stormy weather of the Southern Ocean *Solitaire* leaked through the cockpit lockers into the main hull and was kept afloat by days and nights of endless bailing, the very reading of which sent me to bed with emotionally induced exhaustion. Owing to the paucity of his finances, Leslie's food supply was inadequate in quantity and quality: he finished the voyage on very impoverished rations, losing a great deal of weight and suffering badly from scurvy – *but he got there.*

In discussing heavy-weather sailing with Leslie over a congenial lunch on board *Solitaire* I asked him how he managed to avoid pitchpoling, observing that his boat had a somewhat narrow bow section. He observed that his Hydrovane self-steering gear operated in hurricane-force winds and that he kept the wind firmly on the quarter. Thus the boat will reject the inclination either to roll over or pitchpole. He said, however, that *Solitaire*, a heavy boat, tended to stop in the troughs of big waves, where the water is backward moving and the boat is in the lee of the next wave. *Galway Blazer II*, a light planing boat, would run downwind in a hurricane, her speed off the wave crests did outrun the breakers and carry her on through the ensuing trough. Of course, she finally rolled over when stopped, hove to in the hurricane's aftermath. I think that the safety which stems from keeping moving is due to the fact that if a capsizing situation occurs, you are moving out of it: if you are still, it develops. That has now been generally accepted practice since the analysis of the 1979 Fastnet Storm.

And so I bid you farewell and suggest to you that sailing alone is like life: you are born alone, you die alone and, however gregarious you may be, you have to make your own way through life.

Bibliography

Heavy Weather Sailing, K. Adlard Coles, Adlard Coles, 1967
An Evolution of Single Handers, D. H. Clarke, Stanford Maritime, 1976
A Guide to the Collision Avoidance Rules, 3rd Edition, A. N. Cockcroft and
    J. N. P. Lomeiger, Stanford Maritime, 1965
The Shell Guide to Yacht Navigation, Captain J. Coote, RN, Faber, 1987
La Voile en Solitaire de Slocum à la Transatlantique, Alain Gliksman, Editions
    Maritimes et d'Outre Mer
The Holy Bible (New Testament Gospels)
Dive and Attack, Bill King, William Kimber, 1983
Adventure in Depth, Bill King, Nautical, 1976; Putnam, USA, 1975
Francis Chichester, Anita Leslie, Hutchinson with Hodder and Stoughton,
    1975
The Voyaging Stars, David Lewis, Collins, 1978
'Secrets of the Pacific Island Navigators', David Lewis, T. Oceania
Meteorology for Mariners, MET 0695, Crown, 1978
Hands Open, Leslie Powles, Kenneth Mason, 1987
The Conquest of Happiness, Bertrand Russell, Allen and Unwin, 1930
The History of Western Philosophy, Bertrand Russell, Allen and Unwin, 1946
The S.A.S. Survival Handbook, John Wiseman, Collins Harvill, 1986

Index

LAST SUMMER